How Do AIDS & Society Connect?

Understanding AIDS

Books in This Series

How Do AIDS & Politics Connect?

How Do AIDS & Poverty Connect?

How Do AIDS & Science Connect?

How Do AIDS & Society Connect?

Why Do I Need to Understand AIDS?

Understanding **AIDS**

How Do AIDS & Society Connect?

Sheila Stewart

Village Earth Press

Understanding AIDS
How Do AIDS & Society Connect?

Copyright © 2016 by Village Earth Press, a division of Harding House Publishing. All rights reserved. No part of this publication may be reproduced or transmitted in any form or by any means, electronic or mechanical, including photocopying, recording, taping, or any information storage and retrieval system, without permission from the publisher.

Village Earth Press
www.villageearthpress.com

First Printing
9 8 7 6 5 4 3 2 1

ISBN (paperback): 978-1-62524-399-7
ISBN (paperback series): 978-1-62524-443-7
ISBN (ebook): 978-1-62524-101-6
    Library of Congress Control Number: 2013953519

Author: Stewart, Sheila

Note: This book is a revised and updated edition of *AIDS & Society* (ISBN: 978-1-934970-26-3), published in 2009 by Alpha House Publishing.

Contents

Introduction	6
1. What Is HIV/AIDS?	9
2. What Is Society?	27
3. How Does Society Impact AIDS?	39
4. How Does AIDS Impact Society?	55
5. How Is Society Changing to Support Those with AIDS?	69
For More Information	90
Glossary	92
Bibliography	108
Index	110
Picture Credits	111
About the Author and the Consultant	112

Introduction

What do you know about HIV/AIDS? Where do you get your information? From your friends? From your parents? At school? From television?

You hear a lot about AIDS and HIV these days. But lots of kids—and adults, too—don't really understand HIV/AIDS. They need clearly presented, straightforward facts to replace false information from family and friends and keep themselves safe.

HIV/AIDS is a global epidemic. The facts, from the World Health Organization (WHO) *can be* scary:

- 34 million people were living with HIV/AIDS at the end of 2011.
- 2.5 million people were infected with HIV/AIDS in 2011.
- More than 2/3 of the population of sub-Saharan Africa is infected with HIV/AIDS.
- Over 25 million people have died due to HIV/AIDS in the last 30 years.

No matter how scary the facts seem, they should not overpower us. The world is fighting HIV/AIDS every day at the global and the individual level. There is no cure for HIV, but there are treatments. However, many people in the world continue to go without the treatments they need. The Joint United Nations Programme on HIV/AIDS (UNAIDS) reports that, globally, more than 7 million people that are in need of HIV/AIDS treatment still do not have access. In fact, 72 percent of children with HIV/AIDS do not have access even though they are eligible for treatment. This series talks about what organizations such as the WHO and UNAIDS are doing about the problem.

These books discuss the effects of different aspects of society on the HIV/AIDS pandemic. For example, gender, age, poverty, political struggles, and geography all affect peoples' overall health and access to treatment. In addition, many people, afraid of the social stigma and perceived death sentence of an HIV diagnosis, avoid seeking help when it is needed.

The truth is vital to preventing further spread of the disease. People need to get tested, learn their status, and begin antiretroviral therapy treatment in order to help prevent spreading the disease to others. Education is key to this process of prevention. This series promotes prevention and action through education. The books are intended for distribution to families, libraries, and schools around the world to help reduce fear, increase knowledge, and promote prevention.

The series also touches on what the world is doing to end the HIV/AIDS epidemic and offers suggestions for how readers can get involved at the individual, community, or global level.

—Dr. Elise Berlan

Words to Understand

If something is *acquired*, you get it through something you do (rather than it coming to you through your genes or some other part of your make-up over which you have no control).

Your *immune system* fights off germs and keeps you from getting sick.

A *deficiency* is when you don't have enough of something.

A *syndrome* is a collection of disease symptoms doctors don't completely understand.

Antibodies are special proteins in your blood that fight germs.

If something is *infectious* it can pass from one person to another.

Transfusions are injections of blood or blood components into the bloodstream.

Developed nations are countries where the majority of the population have higher incomes with all the services they need. There are many industries in these countries. Most of Japan, the United States, Canada, Israel, and many of the countries in Europe are all developed countries.

Developing nations are countries where most of the people live in poverty and have few educational, professional, and medical opportunities. Much of the population usually depends on farming for their livelihoods, and there are few industries. Most of the countries of Africa and South America are considered to be developing nations.

A *crisis* is a turning point in life. Often the outcomes of these moments are terrible—but the potential for new growth and a better world is also present in every crisis as well.

Find the Answers in the Text

- What does HIV stand for? What does each word mean?
- What does AIDS stand for and what does each word mean?
- Explain why you won't catch AIDS from a family member who lives in another country.
- Name the continent and the animal where HIV probably started.
- Why do people with AIDS usually die from other diseases?
- List three ways you can catch HIV/AIDS.
- What region of the world has the largest number of people living with AIDS?
- Why do people with hemophilia often need blood transfusions?
- Explain the difference between a developed and a developing nation.
- Describe five ways to make sex safer.

1
What Is HIV/AIDS?

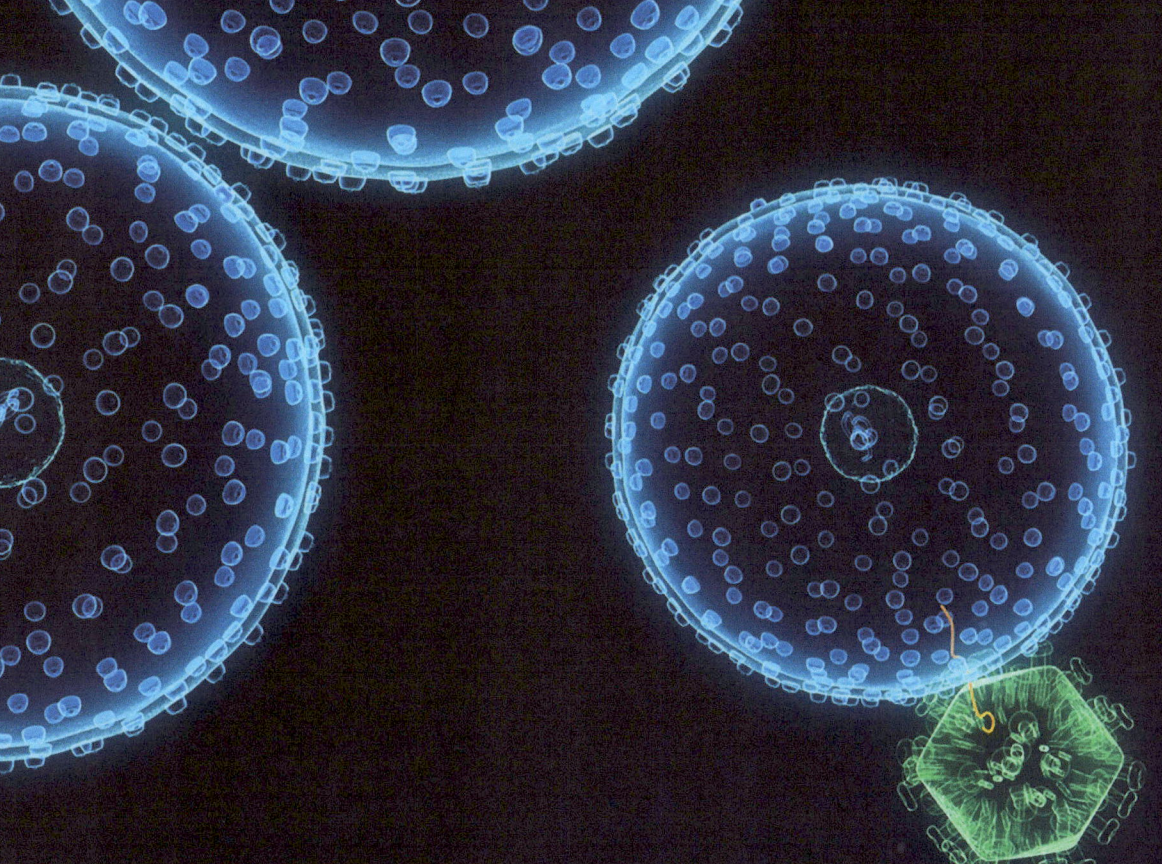

You hear a lot about AIDS and HIV these days. You've probably seen television shows and movies where characters had this disease. You hear about it at school. You may even know someone who has it. You may think it's connected somehow to homosexuals. But lots of kids—and adults too—don't really understand what HIV/AIDS is. They don't know how you catch it, who gets it, or what causes it. Lots of people don't even know what these letters stand for.

HIV stands for human immunodeficiency virus. It's the virus that causes AIDS—acquired immunodeficiency syndrome. People may have the HIV virus in their bodies, and still have no symptoms that they're sick. As the disease becomes worse, though, and people develop symptoms, it often is referred to as AIDS.

Acquired immunodeficiency syndrome—AIDS—got its name because:

- It is *acquired*; in other words, it is a condition that has to be passed to you from another person. It cannot be inherited from your parents or passed along to you by your genes. This means if your boyfriend has HIV/AIDS you could catch it from him—but if your grandmother who lives in another country has HIV/AIDS, you're not going to discover that she passed it on to you.
- It affects the body's *immune system*, the part of the body that fights off diseases.
- It is considered a *deficiency* because it makes the immune system stop working the way it should.
- At first doctors thought it was a *syndrome* because people with AIDS experience a number of different symptoms and diseases. A syndrome is a word doctors use for a collection of symptoms they don't completely understand, and when the term AIDS was first used, doctors only knew about the disease's late stages. They didn't understand exactly what was making people sick. Today, doctors think that "HIV disease" is a better name, but AIDS is still the name that most people use.

Your Immune System

The worst thing about AIDS is that it hurts your immune system—the special cells in your blood that fight off germs and keep you from getting sick. When this happens, you can get sick with other infections, and your body won't be able to fight off the illness. People with AIDS often actually die from another disease (such as an infection caused by a fungus, pneumonia, brain infections, or cancer).

When a virus or bacteria (what we often call germs) get into your body through a cut, through the air you breathe, or through something you've eaten, special white blood cells called helper T cells, also called CD4 lymphocytes, get busy. They pass along the message to another group of white blood cells—B cells—telling them to make the weapons (called *antibodies*) they need to kill the germs. If a virus or bacteria makes its way past the antibodies, it can cause an infection. When that happens, a different type of T cell recognizes the change in the infected cell and kills it. This prevents the infection from spreading. At least this is what is *supposed* to happen.

> **Did You Know?**
>
> Scientists believe that HIV began in chimpanzees in Africa. The virus was probably spread to humans when the chimpanzees were butchered for their meat. Blood from the animals got into the hunters' wounds, spreading the virus to people.

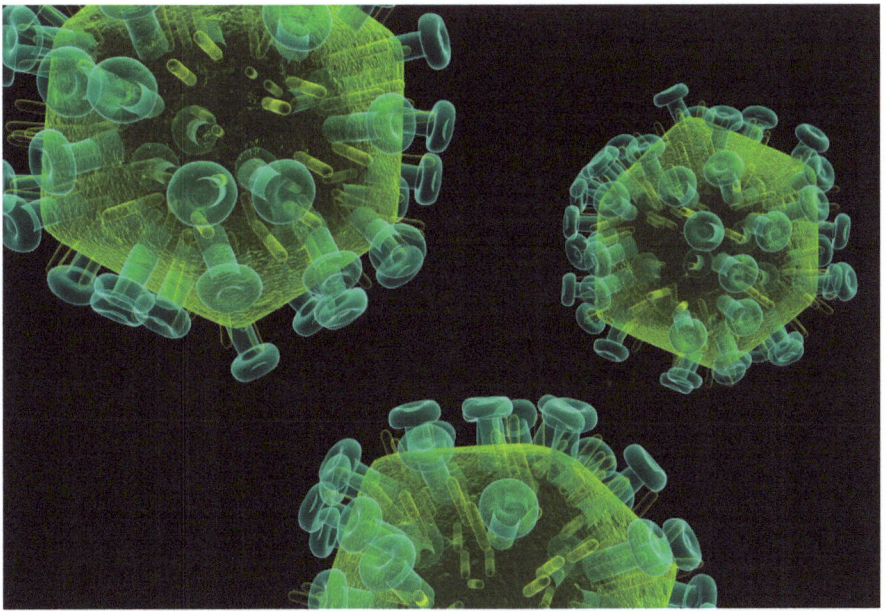

The HIV virus is a tiny organism that needs a host cell in order to act like a living thing. Unlike most living things, viruses have no cells. Instead, they are made mostly of genetic material that changes the cells they infect.

12   how do AIDS & society connect?

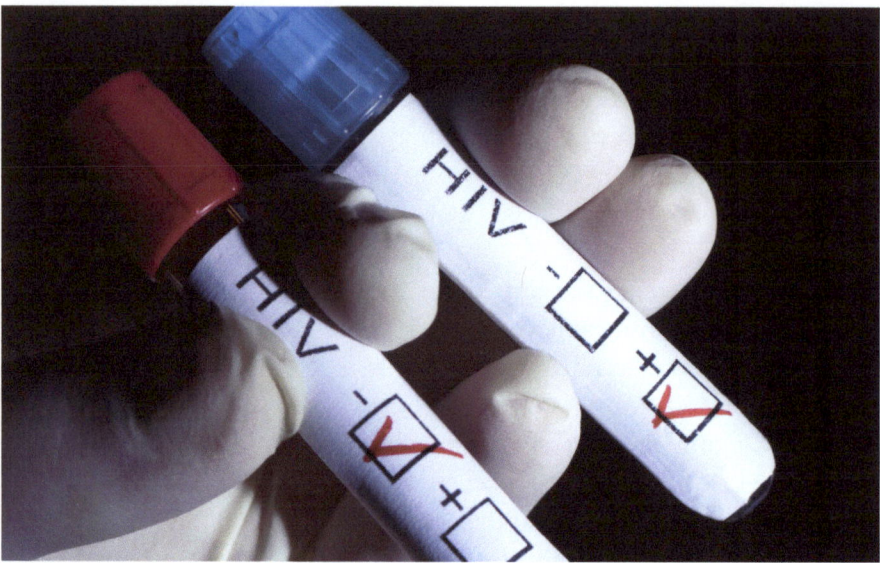

If you think you may have been exposed to the HIV virus, go to your doctor or clinic and get your blood tested. It may be scary to find out the truth—but it's better to know. Even if the news isn't good, new treatments mean that a person with HIV may often live a healthy life for a long time.

When someone has HIV, eventually, she will no longer be able to fight off infections that other people have no problem resisting. As HIV grows within her body, her immune system gets weaker and weaker. She will become more ill more often, especially with certain kinds of cancer and pneumonia.

Doctors say that a person has AIDS when:

- he has tested positive for HIV in his blood.
- he has had one or more AIDS-related infections or illnesses.
- the number of CD4 lymphocytes has reached or fallen below 200 per cubic millimeter of blood (a healthy person's T-cell count ranges between 450 and 1,200).

A few people will have AIDS within a few months from the time they are first exposed to HIV, but that's not usual. In most people, symptoms do not show up for ten to twelve years. It's very important to find out if a person has HIV as soon as possible, because doctors now have medicines that can make most people go even longer before developing AIDS.

The one to three months after a person is first infected with the HIV virus is when that person is most *infectious*. The amount of virus in her system is at its highest and T-cell counts are at their lowest, which means she is most likely to pass along the disease to others. During this time, her body has not had time to react to the virus and produce the cells that will fight the virus. Meanwhile, the virus is reproducing itself within the body.

You can't tell that all this is happening. On the outside, there are no symptoms, and a person who is infected can look and feel perfectly well for many years; he may not even know he is infected. As the immune system gets weaker, however, the person becomes more likely to catch the illnesses that the immune system would normally have been able to fight. As time goes by, he is more likely to become ill more often and develop AIDS.

The Spread of HIV/AIDS

This table shows how many people were living with AIDS in different parts of the world in 2012.

Region	2012
Asia	4.8 million
Eastern Europe	1.4 million
Latin America	1.4 million
North America, Western & Central Europe	2.3 million
Oceania	53,000
Caribbean	230,000
Sub-Saharan Africa	23.5 million
North Africa & Middle East	300,000

14 how do AIDS & society connect?

Did You Know?

Scientists and doctors gave HIV/AIDS its name in the 1980s when the first people started getting sick with it. At the beginning, many patients were homosexual men—which made some people think this was a "homosexual problem"—but before long, doctors realized other people were getting sick with HIV and AIDS too. AIDS is an "everybody problem."

How Does HIV Spread?

First, how does it *not* spread? HIV CANNOT be spread by:

• shaking hands with someone who has HIV/AIDS
• hugging someone who has HIV/AIDS
• sharing eating utensils with someone who has HIV/AIDS
• being in the same room with someone who has HIV/AIDS
• touching something that someone with HIV/AIDS has touched
• breathing the same air as someone with HIV/AIDS

Doctors have never found any cases where someone caught HIV by doing any of these things with a family member, friend, or coworker.

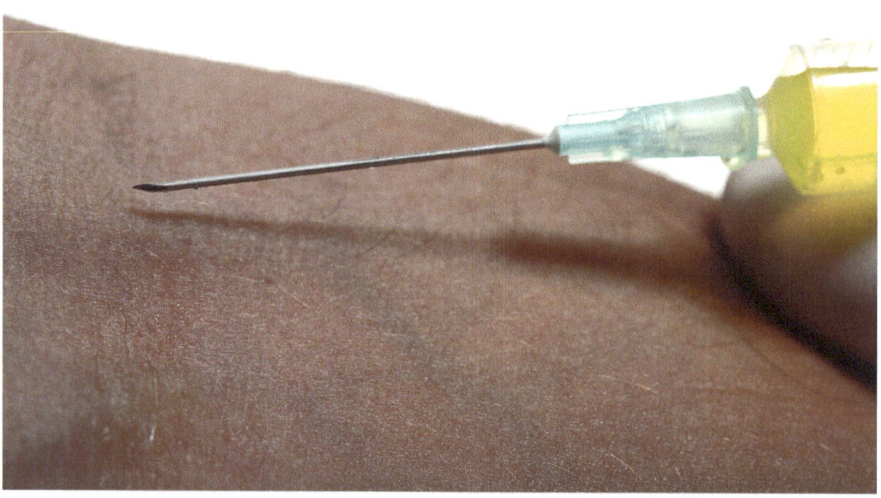

Scientists have found that the HIV virus can survive in needles for more than a month. This means that if you inject drugs with a used needle, you may be shooting HIV into your bloodstream!

Real People

Ryan White began 1984 as a typical thirteen-year-old. He had hemophilia, but it was being treated. He went to school and had friends, just like most kids his age. Then Ryan and his family found out he had caught HIV through the blood products he had received to treat his hemophilia. The HIV had already advanced to AIDS. Doctors told Ryan and his family that he only had six months to live.

Ryan wanted to spend the last months of his life doing what he had been doing, going to school and being with friends. But the school didn't want him there. People were afraid Ryan's illness might "rub off" on the other students. Ryan's battle to be allowed to attend school made news first in the United States and then all over the world. Because of Ryan, people all over the world started thinking about AIDS.

On April 8, 1990, Ryan White lost his battle with AIDS. He was only nineteen when he died, but he had done a lot with his life. Because he fought hard to make people realize that AIDS is a problem we must all face, laws were passed to help people with HIV/AIDS, television shows were made, magazine articles were written, and education programs were started in schools. The world began to work together to fight this terrible disease—all because one young boy was brave enough to take a stand.

16   how do AIDS & society connect?

Did You Know?

The virus that causes AIDS changes quickly. This means that today's medicines may not be able to fight the new strains of HIV.

The ONLY way to become infected with HIV is through certain body fluids. The person infected with the virus carries it in blood, semen, vaginal secretions, and breast milk. In order for you to catch HIV, one of these fluids from a person with HIV would have to enter your bloodstream. Here are the most common ways that HIV could get into your blood:

- during unprotected sex (sex where no condom is used)
- during the kind of drug use where the user "shoots up" with a needle (if the needle is dirty and was used by someone who has HIV)
- through a cut or sore on the skin.

Global Statistics on HIV/AIDS in 2011

Number of people living with HIV

Adults	30.7 million
Women	17.5 million
Children under age 15	3.3 million
Total	34.0 million

People Newly Infected with HIV
(according to UNAIDS research)

Adults	2.2 million
Children under age 15	330,000
Total	2.5 million

AIDS Deaths

Adults	1.5 million
Children under age 15	230,000
Total	1.7 million

The most common way to catch HIV is through unprotected sexual intercourse. This means any kind of sex—oral, anal, or vaginal. Women are more at risk for catching HIV this way than are their male partners, but women can also pass along HIV to men through sexual intercourse.

Some drug users share needles and other equipment. This makes intravenous drug users another group of people who often get HIV. Needles used for body piercing and tattooing can also carry HIV and should not be reused. If you decide to get a piercing or a tattoo, be sure to only have it done by someone who uses only clean equipment.

The youngest people with AIDS—the babies—generally get the disease from their mothers. In most of these cases, the mother does not know she is infected, especially since there can be many years between when she was exposed to the virus and when she first gets symptoms. If there is any chance a woman has been exposed to HIV, she should be tested for the virus before becoming pregnant. Medicine can be given to pregnant women with HIV to protect to their babies during pregnancy. After the baby is born, women with HIV should not breastfeed, so that the virus isn't passed to their babies through breast milk.

Researchers are developing new medicines that are more effective at fighting the HIV virus. Unfortunately, some of the areas of the world that need this medication most are too poor to afford it.

Did You Know?

Less than a hundred years ago, many people died from diseases like smallpox and polio. When researchers created a shot—a vaccine—that keeps people from catching these diseases, they saved millions of lives. One day, scientists hope to discover a vaccine that will protect against HIV/AIDS in the same way.

HIV/AIDS and Blood Transfusions

In the 1970s and early 1980s, before anyone knew very much about HIV/AIDS, blood donors who didn't know they had the disease gave their blood to hospitals and at Red Cross blood drives—and the virus got into the blood supply that was given out to sick or injured people who needed blood *transfusions*. Eventually, doctors realized that some people were catching HIV/AIDS from blood transfusions. Beginning in 1985, the blood supply has been tested for HIV, and there is no longer much risk that someone will get HIV/AIDS from a blood transfusion. However, people who received transfusions between 1975 and 1985 had a high risk of receiving infected blood. Among those most at risk were people with hemophilia.

Hemophilia

Hemophilia is an illness in which blood clots much more slowly than normal. As a result, small cuts and other injuries can cause heavy bleeding. Boys are more apt to have this disease than girls.

People with hemophilia must use blood and blood products to control bleeding episodes. This made them vulnerable to the contaminated blood supply between 1975 and 1985.

Using a condom is one of the best ways to protect yourself against the HIV virus.

Some reports indicate that, during this time, as many as half of the individuals with hemophilia were infected with HIV through blood and blood products. According to the website www.hemophilia.org, an estimated 18,000 people with hemophilia have HIV today.

You cannot get HIV by donating blood. And today, the risk of becoming infected with HIV through the use of blood and blood products is greatly reduced for individuals with hemophilia. More careful screening of blood donors has been one reason for this; blood from every donor is checked for HIV before it is used. New methods of treating the blood and blood products, including the use of heat, have also reduced the risk.

Treatment for HIV/AIDS

Up until recently, if you found out you had HIV, you thought you would die soon. Today, however, some people who have the virus have

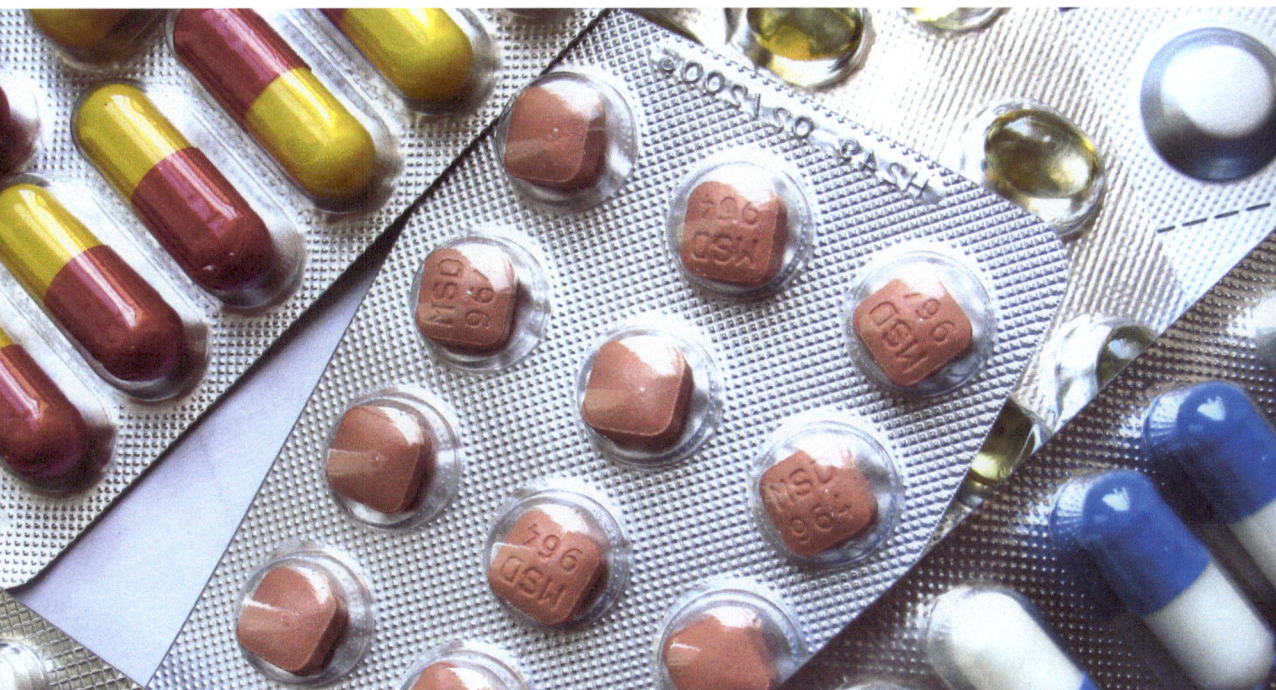

HIV does not respond well to just one single medicine. Instead, doctors have found that the disease responds best to a combination of various medicines. Taking so many pills can be hard to remember—and it's expensive.

how do AIDS & society connect?

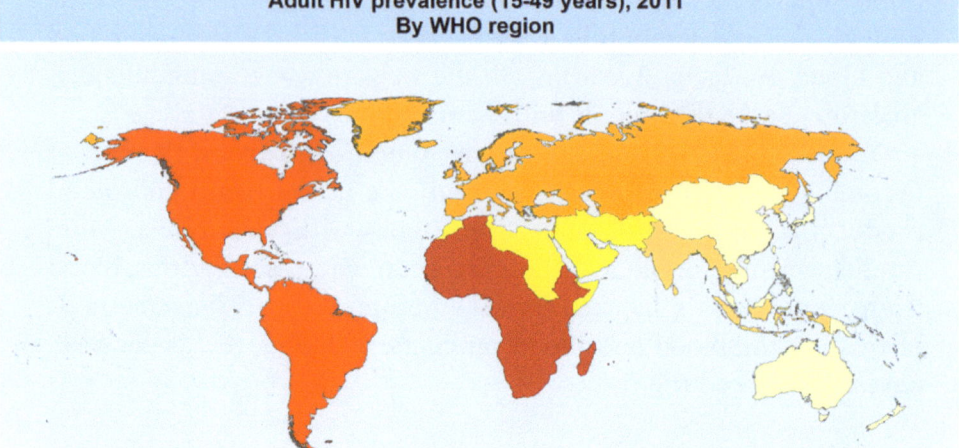

This map created by the World Health Organization (WHO) shows the areas of the world where HIV is most prevalent. Africa has the largest percentage of people living with HIV. Next comes the Americas, then Europe, and next after that is Southeast Asia and the Mediterranean region of the world. China, Australia, Japan, and other nations in the Pacific Ocean have very small percentages of people living with HIV.

still not developed AIDS even after many years. AIDS has no cure yet, but many people with HIV are living longer and staying healthier. New medicines have made this possible.

For many people living with HIV/AIDS, a single medicine does not work. Most take a combination of many drugs, sometimes called a "cocktail." The medicines have to be taken a certain way at certain times in order for them to work. They work together to reduce the level of HIV in the body, allowing the body's own CD4 lymphocytes to return to healthier levels. This is good news. But it doesn't mean that HIV/AIDS is no longer a huge problem in our world today.

For one thing, some people have a hard time remembering when and how to take so many different kinds of medicines. Imagine if you had to take four or more different pills every day at different times throughout the day. You'd probably forget sometimes. So do lots of people who are taking these medicines. But when they do, the medicines don't work as well for them, and new forms of the virus can develop.

The medicines also have some bad side effects. They can damage a person's kidneys, heart, and bones. If this happens, the person cannot keep taking the medicines.

But the worst problem with these medicines is that they are very expensive. Around the world, many of the people living with HIV/AIDS are also living in poverty. They may have no money to buy the medicine or even go to the doctor. They may live in a region so poor that they don't even have a doctor or clinic nearby where they could go if they did have money.

People living with HIV/AIDS in North America, Europe, and other *developed nations* have a better chance of living longer, even when they are poor. Many of these countries have special programs to help bring AIDS medicines to people living in poverty. These programs are not perfect; many times people may make just enough money that they don't qualify, but not enough money that they can afford to buy the medicines on their own. But as researchers find new ways to treat HIV/AIDS, these people may one day have access to better medicine and even a vaccine.

These children in Ethiopia have a high risk of contracting HIV and poverty makes their situation worse.

How Can You Keep Yourself Safe?

The only way to be sure you won't catch HIV/AIDS is to protect yourself from other people's body fluids. Sex is the way most people come into contact with body fluids. So if you don't want to catch HIV/AIDS, you need to protect yourself by not having sex until you are sure it is safe. Women and men don't need to worry about getting HIV/AIDS from each other:

- *if neither partner ever had sex with anyone else.*

- *if neither partner ever shared needles.*

- *if neither partner currently has or ever had HIV/AIDS.*

What Is Safer Sex?

The only way to be absolutely certain you don't catch something from a sexual partner is to not have sex until you know you're in a safe relationship where both of you will keep your promises to be faithful to each other. However, "safer sex" is anything you can do to lower your risk of getting HIV/AIDS (or another disease) if you do choose to have sex outside a safe relationship. The most important ways to reduce your risk are:

- *Keep your partner's body fluids out of your body, including your vagina, anus, or mouth. The body fluids to be most careful about are blood, semen, vaginal fluids, and the runny discharge from sores.*

Safer sex also means protecting your partner:

- *Don't allow your body fluids to get into your partner's body.*

- *Don't have sex if you have sores or other symptoms of infection.*

- *Have routine checkups for sexually transmitted infections.*

- *Get the correct treatment if you become infected.*

When you are a child, it's the job of the adults in your life to protect you and keep you safe. As you get older, though, it will be up to you to protect yourself from danger. Take care of yourself! Make sure you're not one of the millions of people around the world who are living with HIV/AIDS.

Some of the world's *developing nations* don't have even the most basic medicines to treat their people, let along the medications that treat HIV/AIDS. Sometimes the nation's government controls the medicines, and the government decides who gets the medicine, often based on how much money the person has. The big companies that make the medicines are also part of the problem. These companies have often refused to sell drugs at lower prices to the developing world. Clearly, AIDS is an enormous *crisis* in today's society.

Ask the Doctor

Q: My boyfriend and I are careful when we have sex. He always makes sure he pulls out before he comes. My older sister says I can't get pregnant if he does this. Does it also mean I wouldn't catch AIDS from him if he had it?

No! This is not a safe way to protect yourself against either pregnancy or a sexually transmitted infection like HIV/AIDS. During sexual intercourse, a man's penis has a little bit of semen on it even before he ejaculates (or "comes"). Although this is a very small amount, it is enough that you could possibly become pregnant—or get HIV/AIDS from him if he is infected. Latex condoms are the only birth-control method that can also help protect you from HIV/AIDS and other infections. And remember—use condoms correctly with water-based lubricants, to reduce the chance that they could break.

STRAIGHT FROM THE SOURCE

(From the 2004 World Health Organization (WHO) document Protecting Young People from HIV and AIDS.)

Measures to reduce the vulnerability of young people and to reduce risk are complementary and part of a continuum. In terms of the sexual transmission of HIV this is well expressed as:

- DELAY—your first sexual experience,
- REDUCE—the number of your sexual partners,
- PROTECT—yourself and your partner by using a condom.

This approach encourages those who are at no or low risk to remain safe, and encourages all others to move in the direction of greater safety. It helps to create a climate where adolescents can more easily delay the onset of sexual experience, which is the only 100% effective way of avoiding HIV. It addresses the need to reduce the number of sexual partners, since risks rise rapidly with multiple partners. It emphasizes the need for consistent and correct use of condoms. Without condoms, those young people who do not succeed in abstaining are left unprotected at very high risk, and there would be little prospect of reducing HIV levels in the community. Millions of young people would be left to their fate, including girls who are powerless to abstain because sex is forced or coerced. Promoting abstinence and promoting condoms are not alternatives—but complementary parts of an effective approach. Condom use is promoted in order to protect those who are having sex, not to undermine those who are not.

What Do You Think?

- According to this WHO document, what is the only 100 percent effective way to avoid HIV?
- Why do you think the chances of getting HIV go up the more times you have sex with a different person?

- Why do you think some people object to teaching kids about how to use condoms?

- Why do you think other people object to only teaching kids about "abstinence" (not having sex at all)?

- What approach is WHO recommending in this document regarding the condom-abstinence question?

Find Out More

To find out more about HIV/AIDS check out these websites:

Let's Talk: Children, Families, and HIV
www.kidstalkaids.org/education/index.html

YouthAIDS (What You Can Do to Change the World)
www.psi.org/youthaids

Find the Answers in the Text

- What is society? What are the different things we might be referring to when we talk about a society?
- What are some different parts of a person's culture?
- Where does culture come from? Who do you learn it from?
- What is religion?
- How do you decide what to do when your religion, culture, and urban myths give you different information?

Words to Understand

Customs are habitual practices followed by a particular group of people.

Traditions are long-established practices that a society passes down from generation to generation.

A *taboo* is a moral ban placed on a particular action or topic as a result of a society's customs and traditions.

Symbols are signs or tokens that have taken on other long-established meanings within a particular society.

A *deity* is a god associated with one's religious beliefs.

Honor killings are murders committed by family members against women who are accused of bringing shame to the family.

Evangelical has to do with Christian denominations that believe in being "born again" through a personal conversion experience.

2
What Is Society?

how do AIDS & society connect?

You are part of society. You interact with the people around you every day, talking to them, laughing with them, fighting with them. Even when you choose not to interact with people, you are still a member of society.

Society is simply the name for a group of people living in a community. The word *society* might refer to people from:

- a country—like Australian society
- a region—like European society
- a cultural background—like Western society
- a certain religion—like Muslim society

Culture

Although all human beings share basic things in common, things which make them more alike than they are different, societies vary.

Societies are small human worlds, each with their own rules and traditions. From someone looking in from the outside, those rules and customs may seem strange—but those who live within the society probably take them for granted to the point that they seem almost invisible. Societal traditions are just "the way things are."

What makes societies different from each other are their cultures. Culture involves all the *customs*, beliefs, *traditions*, and behaviors that are shared by a group of people. These can include things like styles of clothing, typical foods, or slang. Culture also includes the things people believe are *taboo* and the way they interpret *symbols*. Whether you wear black to a funeral, like most of Western society, or white, like parts of Asia and Africa, is part of your culture. So is how much skin you cover with clothing; how old you are when you marry (or first have sex); and whether you think a tattoo is an interesting fashion statement, a mark of adulthood, or a horrible thing to do to your body.

> **Did You Know?**
>
> *Personal space—the amount of space a person needs between herself and another person to feel comfortable—is different in different cultures. Americans tend to like a lot of space when talking to someone they don't know well, while people from South America or the Mediterranean would probably stand a lot closer together.*

From the moment you were born, you began absorbing the culture around you. You did this by watching other people, by listening, and when you were old enough, by reading. By the time you were ready to

Without realizing it, every minute of every day, children are naturally absorbing their culture from the adults around them, especially their parents.

> **Did You Know?**
>
> *Urban legends—those wild stories about the dangers of cell phones or alligators living in the sewers—have been around a lot longer than e-mail. People have been telling stories since the beginning of history. Some of the stories are true, some are exaggerated, and some are just completely made up. But just because you got the information from your best friend who would never lie to you doesn't necessarily mean it's true. If it's important, it's worth checking out.*

start school, you already knew a lot about your society and your place in it. Most of what you knew, you had soaked up without realizing. Even now, you've probably never really thought closely about why you think the way you do about a lot of things. Things you think about as "the way things are" might actually be specific to your society. If you've lived most of your life in the United States or Canada, for example, you might guess that someone not wearing a ring on the fourth finger of her left hand is unmarried. But while this might be true in a number of countries, in many others the wedding ring is worn on the right hand. And in India, a toe ring is often worn instead.

Religion

Even if you don't think of yourself as a religious person, religion affects you. For one thing, religion is not just about going to church or temple or mosque. A person's religion has to do with the ideas he has about a *deity*, as well as the ideas he has about moral questions. Even if a person believes there is no God, this is still a religious belief. And you are influenced by the religious ideas in the society around you, even when you aren't aware of it.

Different societies and cultures have different religious beliefs. Even when religious beliefs overlap, societies often differ in how much they value or condemn a behavior. For example, while having sex outside of marriage is frowned on by a number of religions, the consequences can range from stern lectures, divorce (in the case of adultery), forced marriage (in the case of premarital sex), or, very rarely, beatings or *honor killings*.

The connections between religion and culture can be complicated. Many times behaviors (such as honor killings, for instance) are interpreted by people as being religious, when in fact they are condemned by that religion. People not part of a religion frequently make judgments about that religion's beliefs which are not true, because they do not know very much about it. On the other hand, though, people who are members of a religion also assume some practices or beliefs are part of their religion when they are not. (For example, some *Evangelical* Christians might believe that not drinking alcohol is a religious practice, when in fact it may be merely cultural.) People can confuse cultural practices with religious teachings, but this does not change the influence they have on society.

Everyone has habits, and those habits can be very hard to change. If you've ever tried to stop biting your fingernails or putting jobs off until the last minute, you know how hard it can be to change your habits. People often like to sit in the same seat on the school bus every day, order the same meals at restaurants, or go into the mall through the same entrance. There's usually nothing wrong with these things; they just mean that a lot of people feel comfortable when they follow routines.

Easter eggs, the Easter Bunny, and Easter baskets are traditions that are celebrated in many countries of the world, especially those with a European heritage. In today's world, few people may remember what eggs, a bunny, and a basket have to do with Easter (or with each other)—and yet they take for granted that these are symbols of this springtime holiday.

> **Ask the Doctor**
>
> Q. My friend's cousin told her that if she douched with bleach after sex she couldn't get AIDS, because the bleach would kill the virus. Is that true?
>
> No, not at all. Bleach can burn your skin, and using bleach as a douche could seriously injure you. But douching with anything, in fact, is not an effective way to prevent any sexually transmitted infections (or pregnancy, for that matter).

Traditions are a little like the habits of an entire society. They are "the ways things have always been done:" the ideas, beliefs, and actions that are passed down from generation to generation. Sometimes individual families develop their own traditions, and sometimes a larger part of society follows traditions. For example, it's the tradition of most Christians in Western society to celebrate Christmas on December 25, while those in countries like Russia celebrate it on January 7.

Like habits, traditions can be hard to change. In some societies, for instance, slavery has traditionally been practiced. People in those societies are used to the idea of having slaves. For them, slavery is simply "the way things are" and "the way things have always been done." When more and more people realize that slavery should not be "the way things are," the society can begin to change, but the process is usually long and painful. And even after the practice of slavery has been ended, the attitudes and beliefs associated with slavery often remain as part of that society for much longer. Traditional beliefs can be very hard to change because people do not usually think about them.

Myths and Facts

The word "myth" is often used to describe a story that many people believe is true but which is, in fact, false. Sometimes a myth is a story that helps people make sense of the world; it can be true without being literally factual. Figuring out which of society's beliefs are myths and which are facts can be difficult.

We live in a society that is full of information. The Internet allows both factual information and a society's myths to be passed along quickly and easily. You might also get some of your beliefs and ideas from your parents, your teachers, your friends, or an e-mail someone forwarded to you. Which of these sources is most reliable? Which do you personally trust the most?

People in Western cultures traditionally wear black to symbolize their sadness and mourning over the death of a loved one.

34 how do AIDS & society connect?

In many Asian cultures, white was once worn to represent mourning. Today, it is more common to see funeral attendees in black, a custom adopted from Western cultures.

So how do you know what to believe?

Education is the best answer to that question. Some of our traditions and beliefs—like which hand you wear your wedding ring on or which day you celebrate Christmas—don't make much of a difference to our life and health, but others could make all the difference in the world.

HIV/AIDS is one of those topics about which people often have a lot of wrong ideas. Because people worry about ways they might accidentally catch HIV, they come up with ideas about how to prevent infection. These methods of protection may actually expose them to greater risk—or they may become the basis for needless discrimination against people with AIDS. Learning the facts about HIV/AIDS can help you make smart decisions, without living your life in fear.

A society's culture and traditions can affect the spread of HIV/AIDS as well. AIDS is a global problem and all across the world people are working to prevent more infections and to treat all those who are already infected with HIV. The challenges in meeting this goal are different for different societies.

STRAIGHT FROM THE SOURCE

(From Richard M. Alston's The Individual vs. the Public Interest.*)*

The Meaning of Society

Society must be understood as a combination of functional, cognitive, and cultural systems. Functional systems include market, political, institutional, and familial processes and deal with the production and consumption of goods, the provision of services, the waging of war, and the administration of justice and education. Cognitive systems organize values to guide choice among alternatives. A unique combination of functional, cognitive, and cultural systems defines and distinguishes a society.

The society changes as any element within it changes and the process of change is constant. Values are preached and rejected, technology is altered, roles are achieved. Change creates stress, but adaptation and adjustment make possible continuity (and perhaps a temporary stability). Thus, a society may experience significant change in its functional system through a political or technological revolution, yet still maintain its essential quality. The force that holds it together, that gives society meaning, in spite of change, is ideology.

An ideology is a way of looking at the world that is shared by members of a group; it connects individual precepts to those generally held in the society and provides the group a base for consensus.

Ideological change on a large scale is revolution. There is a significant difference between the evolutionary change that constantly marks society, and revolutionary change that literally transforms the society into something new, something not previously experienced by the individuals within it. Such revolutionary change comes about when the cognitive, cultural, and functional systems have accumulated so much change, together or independently, that they are no longer commensurate with the ideology that served to interpret them. When the problems confronted no longer seem capable of solution within the existing systems of information organization—then comes revolutionary change.

What Do You Think?

- According to this author, what functions does ideology serve within a society?

- How does this author define a revolution?

- How has the AIDS epidemic changed our society? Do you think it has brought about a revolution? Why or why not?

Find Out More

To find out more about society, culture, and traditions around the world, check out these websites:

Culture Quest
www.ipl.org/div/cquest

Family Traditions
www.americanfamilytraditions.com/traditions_customs_rituals.htm

Social Customs, Traditions, and Folklore
www.ipl.org/IPLBrowse/GetSubject?vid=13&cid=4&tid=7193&parent=6687

Find the Answers in the Text

- How do societal structures contribute to the spread and treatment of HIV/AIDS?
- In chapter 1, you learned that HIV could be spread through semen. How does a society's attitude toward sex play a role in the spread of HIV?
- How does drug use affect the spread of HIV?
- How does it affect the spread of HIV/AIDS when a society looks down on those who have the disease and treat them as if they are lower-class citizens?

Words to Understand

To *eradicate* means to do away with something completely.

Mainstream refers to the part of something considered to be the most active, as well as the trends, thoughts, and actions that go along with that part.

Hypocrisy means pretending to be or feel something other than what you actually are or feel.

Monogamous refers to a sexual relationship with only one partner.

Promiscuous refers to people who engage in sexual activity with many sexual partners.

Something that is *anonymous* takes place without names or identities being revealed.

Sanctioned means based upon or authorized by law or traditional rules.

A person who is *marginalized* is excluded or ignored by being pushed to the edges of a society.

A *stigma* is a mark of shame or disgrace.

Discrimination is when one group of people is treated differently from others within a society.

Harassed means continually persecuted or tormented.

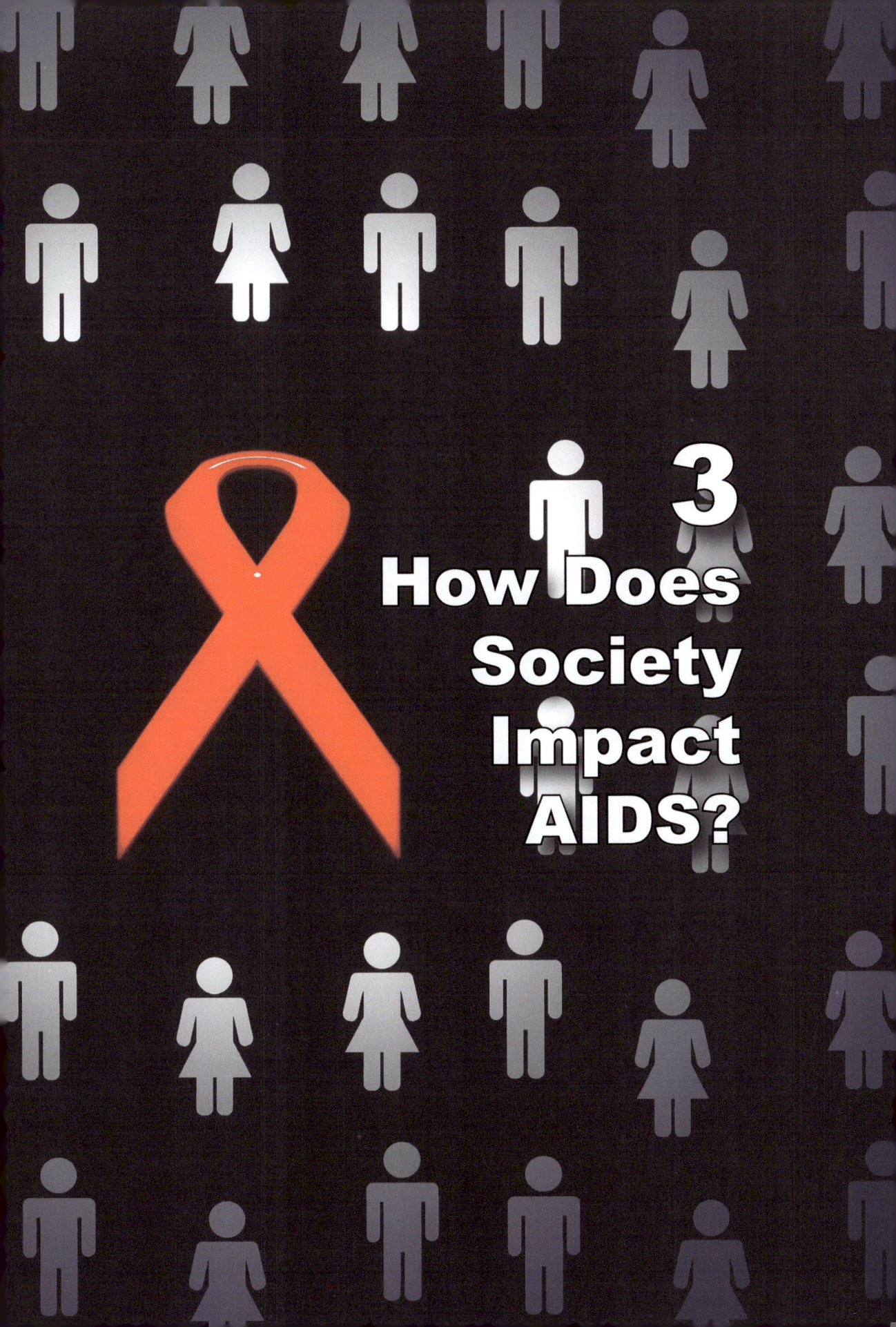
3
How Does Society Impact AIDS?

40 how do AIDS & society connect?

Every society has its good points and its bad points, its own set of benefits and advantages, problems and challenges. This is also true when it comes to the fight against AIDS. While people everywhere want to *eradicate* HIV/AIDS, some societies are more at risk for the spread of the disease than others.

So why is that? What makes certain societies more vulnerable to AIDS?

There are a lot of different answers to that question. Although societies' customs and traditions shouldn't be thought of as "bad" or "good," they can sometimes lead to conditions that make it more difficult to control the spread of HIV/AIDS. Because cultures are made up of complex patterns of traditions, beliefs, and practices, it can be very hard at times to figure out how to resolve these issues.

Sexual Practices

Since HIV/AIDS is most often spread through sexual contact, it makes sense that society's ideas about sex seriously affect the spread of AIDS.

Because the first people in North America to be diagnosed with AIDS were homosexual men, doctors first thought only homosexuals were susceptible to the disease. When scientists discovered HIV was a virus that could be transmitted through blood, semen, or breast milk, they quickly realized

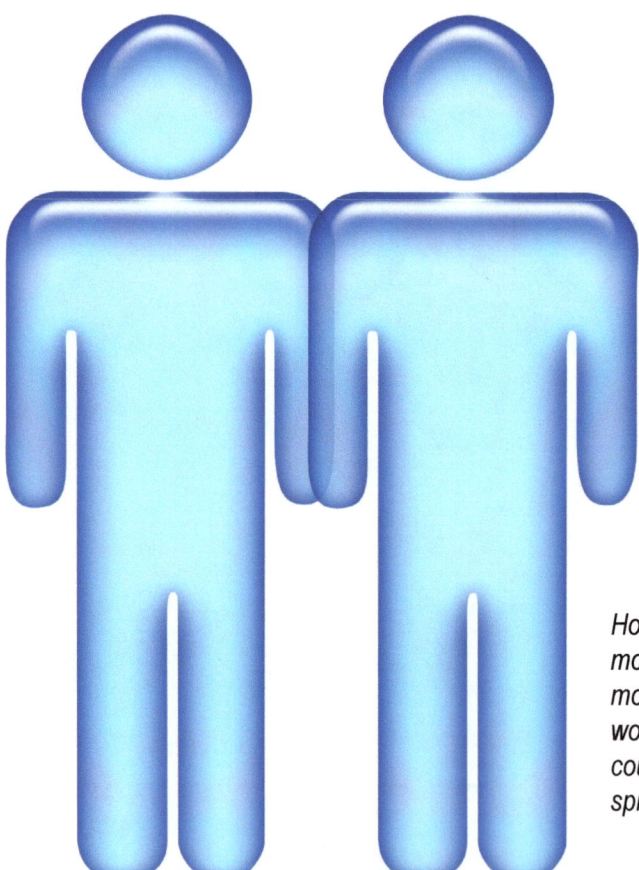

Homosexual males in committed monogamous relationships are no more likely to catch or spread HIV than would a heterosexual monogamous couple. It is not homosexuals that spread HIV but promiscuity.

that anyone who came into contact with these fluids was at risk for developing AIDS—but even though doctors and researchers knew in the early 1980s how HIV was transmitted, the public perception remained for a long time that only homosexuals got AIDS. For this reason, many people thought that as long as they only had heterosexual sex, they were safe. They didn't worry about taking precautions against HIV/AIDS, and some of them were infected as a result.

Meanwhile, North American homosexual society's customs and behaviors may have made it initially susceptible to spreading HIV/AIDS. During the 1970s and 1980s, many American gay men "came out" and openly embraced their homosexuality, forming communities, especially in San Francisco on the West Coast and New York City on the East. At the same time, *mainstream* American society rejected homosexual society. This meant that homosexual males often lived their lives without older role models, outside the traditions that acted as sexual safeguards for much of the rest of society. They often saw themselves as rebels who had been freed from "straight" society's restrictions and *hypocrisy*. Gay males celebrated their sexuality not

Gay Pride was a movement that began in San Francisco in the 1970s, which was based on three main premises: that people should be proud of their sexual orientation and gender identity, that sexual diversity is a gift, and that sexual orientation and gender identity are inherent and cannot be intentionally altered. The rainbow flag is the symbol of this movement.

42 how do AIDS & society connect?

HIV spreads more quickly in societies that condone multiple sexual partners for each person.

with the *monogamous* committed relationships idealized by mainstream society but with *promiscuous* and often *anonymous* sex; in other words they had lots of sex with lots of partners—and they often knew next to nothing about the people with whom they were having sex. This presented an ideal set of societal behaviors for passing along HIV quickly from man to man.

Of course heterosexuals who engage in similar behaviors are just as likely to catch and spread HIV. In some African countries, for example, societal traditions allow husbands to continue to engage in sex with many partners besides their wives. Many of these men travel from their homes in rural areas to find work in cities; while they are away from their wives, they have sex with prostitutes, women who also migrated to the cities seeking to support themselves and turned to prostitution because they lacked other options. When the men go back home, they often bring HIV with them, sharing their infection with their wives. Similarly, the African nation of Zaire has a period

> **Did You Know?**
>
> *Iran has legalized sterile needle exchange programs, a practical approach to limiting the infectious spread of HIV. Other nations refuse to fund such programs through either international or domestic HIV/AIDS prevention programs because such a practice seems to condone heroin use.*

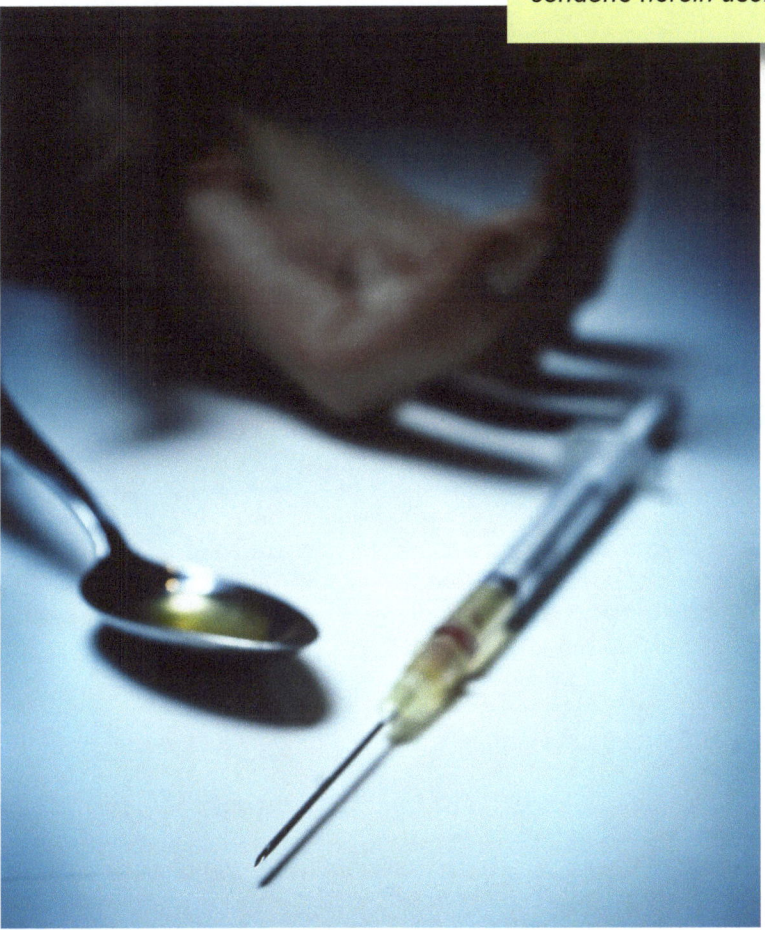

The practice of sharing needles among heroin users has been a major source of the spread of HIV infection.

> **Did You Know?**
>
> *Data gathered on Eastern Europe and Central Asia showed that more than 80 percent of HIV cases were due to intravenous drug use.*

following puberty and before marriage when sexual relations between young men and a number of eligible women are *sanctioned* by society; these young people are also experiencing higher rates of HIV and AIDS.

Societies that lack education about safer sex (whether homosexual or heterosexual) contribute to the spread of HIV. Keep in mind, though, that although promiscuity is considered "bad" in some societies, there are often other reasons for this besides morals and religion. For instance, in Western culture, where inheritance was passed along from father to son, husbands wanted to be sure their sons were biologically theirs; traditions that ensured this discouraged multiple sexual partners. In some regions of Africa, however, family wealth is inherited by the offspring of the mother's uncle rather than by the husband's children. This tradition reduces the societal pressure that discourages promiscuity.

> **How Can You Keep Yourself Safe?**
>
> *According to AVERT, an international AIDS charity organization, sexually transmitted infections often trigger strong societal responses and reactions. From early in the AIDS epidemic, states the AVERT Web site, a series of powerful images were used that reinforced stigmas and made them "okay" in the minds of many people. These images were based on the following assumptions:*
> - *HIV/AIDS was a punishment for immoral behavior.*
> - *HIV/AIDS was a crime.*
> - *HIV/AIDS was a war against a virus (rather than individuals in need of help).*
> - *HIV/AIDS was a horror, in which infected people were demonized and feared.*
> - *HIV/AIDS was based on otherness, in which the disease is an affliction of those set apart from the rest of society. (It affects "them," not "us.")*

Intravenous Drug Use

Because HIV is spread through semen, vaginal fluids, and blood, sexual transmission was the disease's first wave; its second wave was IV drug use, which spreads HIV through blood and dirty needles.

Did You Know?

According to WHO, in 2008, almost 16 million people in the world injected drugs into their bodies, and 3 million of them had HIV.

People who live outside society's mainstream often lack the protections and benefits experienced by other society members. Homosexuals, drug users, and people with HIV/AIDS are often marginalized in this way.

Researchers have found that people who live along heroin trafficking land routes and shipping ports account for much of this second wave of the AIDS epidemic. The flood of heroin through a country tends to increase the number of drug users there who decide that needle injection is the best way to use drugs. This trend is showing up in countries around the world, including Kenya, Tanzania, Turkey, Iran, and China.

Drug users may belong to their own society that normalizes drug use, including IV drug use, thus contributing to the spread of HIV—but mainstream society also contributes to this trend. In most countries around the world, heroin is an illegal substance; this means that heroin users are considered criminals. Users may be reluctant to seek treatment for their habit when doing so could lead to criminal charges. This means that like male homosexuals in the 1970s and '80s, drug users are often *marginalized*, forced to live their lives outside the guidelines that both restrict and shelter the larger society.

Mainstream societies can also have a positive effects, however. For example, Iranian public health officials use their society's cultural strengths to confront IV drug use: since the mother in the Iranian family runs the household, health officials have involved mothers with monitoring their children's adherence to drug treatment programs.

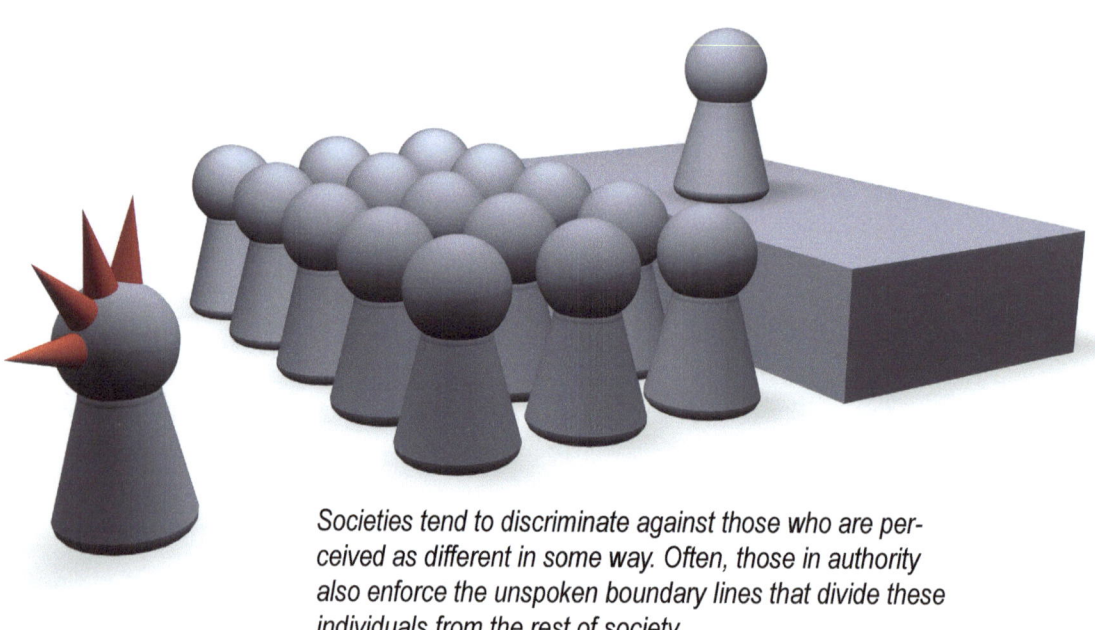

Societies tend to discriminate against those who are perceived as different in some way. Often, those in authority also enforce the unspoken boundary lines that divide these individuals from the rest of society.

Real People

My foster son, Michael, aged 8, was born HIV-positive and diagnosed with AIDS at the age of 8 months. I took him into our family home, in a small village in the southwest of England. At first relations with the local school were wonderful and Michael thrived there. Only the head teacher and Michael's personal class assistant knew of his illness.

Then someone broke the confidentiality and told a parent that Michael had AIDS. That parent, of course, told all the others. This caused such panic and hostility that we were forced to move out of the area. The risk is to Michael and us, his family. Mob rule is dangerous. Ignorance about HIV means that people are frightened. And frightened people do not behave rationally. We could well be driven out of our home yet again.

(Debbie, speaking to the National AIDS Trust, UK, 2002)

Stigma and Misperceptions

Stigma is a social tool that's used to marginalize and exclude individuals with certain characteristics. Think about the kid in grade school no one liked. She may have dressed differently from the rest of you; she probably looked and acted "funny" in some way. Because of those differences, she was an outsider, someone who stood on the sidelines when teams were being picked, who ate lunch alone in the cafeteria, who sat by herself on the playground. She bore the stigma of being different.

In Western societies, illegitimate children and unwed mothers were once on the receiving end of society's rejection. So were homosexuals, drug users, and sex workers. These people lived outside society's approved boundaries. When AIDS came along, it merely reinforced many of society's already existing stigmas. Some people even believed that AIDS was proof that God also disapproved of these groups of people and was punishing them.

From the moment that AIDS made news for the first time back in the 1980s, society responded with fear, denial, stigma, and **discrimination**. Communities, coworkers, schools, and even families and loved ones often rejected people with HIV.

By blaming this group of people for its suffering, society could excuse itself from the responsibility of caring for them.

In some societies, laws and policies increase the stigmatization of people living with HIV/AIDS; compulsory screening and testing for certain jobs, as well as limitations on international travel and migration are all examples of this. Doctors and scientists don't believe that HIV can be transmitted in the workplace, and yet numerous employers have terminated or refused employment to those with HIV. The head of a human resource department in India told United Nations

Job applicants may be turned away if an employer knows he or she has HIV.

workers, "Though we do not have a policy so far, I can say that if at the time of recruitment there is a person with HIV, I will not take him. I'll certainly not buy a problem for the company. I see recruitment as a buying-selling relationship. If I don't find the product attractive, I'll not buy it." Individuals like this justify their actions by saying they're simply doing what's "good for business," or that they're protecting the well-being of other employees. Societies as a whole justify such practices on the grounds that HIV poses a public health risk, but experts believe that in reality, all these laws do is give the public a false sense of security by further marginalizing people with HIV/AIDS.

> **Did You Know?**
>
> According to a survey done in 2009 by the Kaiser Family Foundation, 51 percent of people stated that they would be uncomfortable having someone with HIV prepare their food, and 42 percent stated that they would be uncomfortable having a roommate that was HIV-positive.

People with HIV are often *harassed* by other community members, and AIDS-related murders have been reported in countries around the world, including Brazil, Colombia, Ethiopia, India, South America, and Thailand. "Nobody will come near me, eat with me in the canteen, nobody will want to work with me, I am an outcast here," an HIV-positive man in India told United Nations workers.

This discrimination is not only a violation of individuals' most basic rights to be treated with compassion and respect, but it also interferes with these individuals' access to treatment. Health care facilities may also discriminate against people with HIV. Fearing that they will be infected with contaminated blood, doctors, nurses, and other hospital personnel may refuse to treat patients with the virus. In some parts of the world, even medical professionals are ignorant of how HIV is passed from person to person, and so they do not understand the steps they could take to protect themselves from infection; their discrimination is fueled by fear. A senior doctor from a public hospital in India told UN workers, "There is an almost hysterical kind of fear … at all levels, starting from the humblest, the sweeper or the ward boy, up to the heads of departments, which makes them pathologically scared of having to deal with an HIV-positive patient. Wherever they have an HIV patient, the responses are shameful."

Lack of health-care confidentiality is another right often denied to people with HIV. Many times, these people do not get to choose how, when, and to whom they disclose their HIV status; instead, health-care facilities make this decision for them. Different nations have different regulations regarding this issue, and differences even exist between health-care facilities within the same country. Although legislation in many Western nations, including the United States, Canada, and the UK, protects patient rights, this is not the case in many developing countries. In some hospitals, signs are placed next to patients with HIV, labeling them as "HIV-positive" or simply "AIDS."

Societal stigma has helped magnify the AIDS epidemic. Fear of facing discrimination prevents people with the virus from seeking treatment, which means that more people die. Denial and prejudice gets in the way of education that explains how HIV is transmitted,

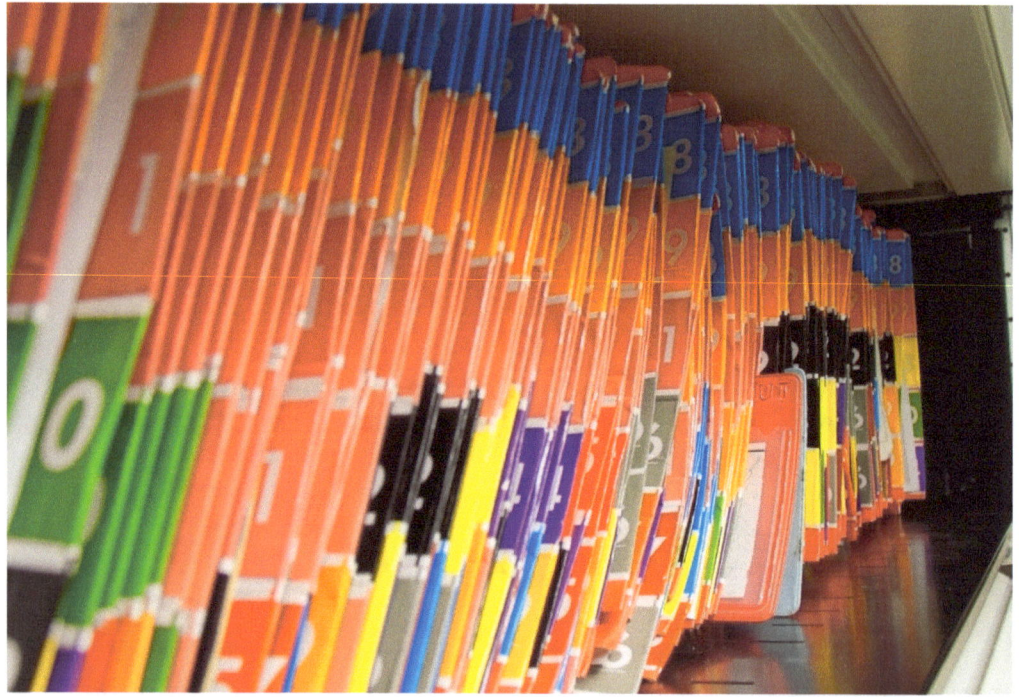

In the United States, the Health Insurance Portability and Accountability Act of 1996 (HIPAA) requires physicians to ensure they are protecting the privacy and security of all patients' medical information, including those with HIV. In the UK, the Confidentiality Code of Practice also protects patients' privacy. In many developing nations, however, patients have no such legal protections.

which means more people will get this disease because they are ignorant as to how to protect themselves. Legislators are reluctant to spend public funds on AIDS research, which means that an answer to this terrible disease has still not been found.

On the other hand, many countries have passed laws that protect the rights of people living with HIV/AIDS, including their rights to privacy and confidentiality, employment, education, and treatment. Education can help spread the word to people living with HIV that they do in fact have legal rights.

However, no government policy, law, or classroom curriculum alone can wipe HIV stigma from the world's societies. Individuals need to take a stand and speak out on behalf of those who are living with this disease. After all, societies are simply groups of individuals—and societies can change, one individual at a time.

> **Did You Know?**
>
> In one survey, 29 percent of persons with HIV/AIDS in India, 38 percent in Indonesia, and over 40 percent in Thailand said their HIV-positive status had been revealed to someone else without their consent.

STRAIGHT FROM THE SOURCE

(From the UNAIDS Web site)

A variety of social and economic factors increase people's vulnerability to HIV infection, including stigma and discrimination, poverty and lack of HIV awareness and access to education, health and other services.

When these factors exist, some people engage in behaviors such as unprotected sex or exchange of contaminated needles that put them at higher risk of becoming infected. These communities include men who have sex with men, people who use injection drugs, and sex workers. The HIV-related stigma adds to the existing negative attitudes that people might have towards them. Frequently, countries have laws that criminalize their behaviors and make it difficult for them to exercise their human rights, including accessing health services.

The resources that are devoted to HIV prevention, treatment and care for these populations are often not proportional to the HIV prevalence among them—this is not only a mismanagement of resources but also a failure to respect fundamental human rights.

In many areas of the world, the HIV epidemic has had a serious effect on human development, undermining progress towards the United Nations Millennium Development Goals, particularly those related to poverty reduction, achieving universal primary education, promoting gender equality, reducing child mortality and improving the health of mothers. This, in turn, has left people who are already vulnerable, such as women and girls, young people and children, refugees and internally displaced persons, and people who migrate among others, at even higher risk of acquiring HIV.

The global and national response to HIV must address the underlying social and structural issues that increase the vulnerability of people and also scale-up HIV-related programs and services for the most affected communities.

What Do You Think?

- According to this document, what factors make people more vulnerable to HIV?

- Does the document indicate that it is individuals' fault that they are vulnerable to HIV transmission—or society's? Do you agree? Why or why not?

- Why do you think women, girls, children, and people who are not settled in one place are more at risk of catching HIV?

Find Out More

Check out these websites to find out more about the ways that society has an impact on AIDS:

The Black Aids Institute
www.blackaids.org

UN Report: "Some African cultural traditions influence spread of AIDS"
www.un.org/apps/news/story.asp?NewsID=26945#.Ud2plj771r4

HIV/AIDS: Risk Factors
www.mayoclinic.com/health/hiv-aids/DS00005/DSECTION=risk-factors

Here's what you need to know

- How do HIV and AIDS affect those living in poverty? How does poverty affect HIV/AIDS?
- How does HIV/AIDS affect the cost of medicine?
- How does HIV/AIDS affect the level and quality of food consumption?
- How does HIV/AIDS affect educational opportunities?

Words to Understand

Prevalent refers to something that is generally found at the present time.

A *pandemic* is a disease outbreak that becomes very widespread and affects a whole region, a continent, or the world.

Economic refers to the production and management of material wealth.

> **Did You Know?**
>
> In 2011, California had the highest number of diagnoses of HIV infection with 5,973 new cases. Florida was next with 5,403 diagnoses, and Texas was third with 5,065 cases.

Imagine you live in a country where more than a third of the population has HIV/AIDS. This means that out of every three people you know, at least one is probably sick. Your teacher has HIV/AIDS, the woman who works in the store where you buy food has HIV/AIDS, and the man who lives next door has it too. Your older brother is sick with the disease, so is his girlfriend, and many of their friends are as well. Everywhere you turn, people are sick and dying. And now your family has just found out your mother and father have HIV/AIDS too.

It sounds like a bad dream, doesn't it, or a movie about some futuristic disaster? But this is a reality for many young adults growing up in Africa. Imagine how this would feel if it were happening to you personally; now magnify that by the number of all the people who live in that society. Societies are reeling from the blows AIDS strikes. When so many people are sick and dying—and the ones who aren't sick are coping with the grief and work of coping with life without their loved ones—societies cannot function as they once did. Schools, stores, churches, hospitals, and homes are all changed.

In nations where HIV/AIDS is not so *prevalent*, the changes the disease has brought to society may not be as noticeable, but they are still real. HIV/AIDS has an enormous affect on societies.

The United Nations (UN) has studied those changes so that the world can better understand what needs to be done to help nations cope with this *pandemic*. The UN found that HIV/AIDS affects societies on many levels in many ways.

Poverty

In many developing nations, households affected by HIV/AIDS often move from a comfortable lifestyle into poverty. Studies in Burundi, Côte d'Ivoire, Haiti, and Zambia showed that many changes occurred in the AIDS-affected households, including loss of paid employment, increased borrowing, and the sale of possessions; in Thailand, one third of households affected by HIV/AIDS had an average decrease in household income of 48 percent. People who are sick can't work, and this loss of income is one of AIDS' heaviest societal burdens.

Medical and Health Concerns

In developing and developed nations, the AIDS pandemic has had an effect on the medical world. In the United States in particular, HIV/AIDS has contributed to sexuality being considered a medical issue, one which now engages the attention of health professionals (where in the past this was not as true). On the one hand, the search

The homeless and people who live in poverty have poor nutrition, inadequate health care, and fewer educational opportunities. This puts them at greater risk of catching HIV. Once a person has HIV, he is also more likely to drop below the poverty level, at which point, homelessness is just one of the many risks he faces.

Did You Know?

According to a report in 2010, the funding for HIV/AIDS programs could cost anywhere between $400 billion to $700 billion over the next twenty years.

for a cure has brought new passion to the field of medical research, but the cost of researching, preventing, containing, and treating HIV also puts a strain on medical system resources.

Around the world, in both developed and developing nations, households with someone with HIV/AIDS have to spend more money on doctor's bills and

Children who live in households where at least one member has HIV/AIDS have less food. The food they do eat is more apt to be a cheap carbohydrate such as rice, which does not provide them with all the nutrients they need.

medicines. HIV/AIDS-related illnesses put a heavy financial burden on households affected by the epidemic.

Food Consumption

People in many HIV/AIDS-affected households don't eat as much. This may be because there's not enough money to buy the food they need, or because the people in the household who once grew the food are now too sick to work on the land. Mothers who are sick may be too weak and tired to purchase and prepare food. The change in food intake leads to malnutrition, especially among children. Malnutrition then makes these kids and adults more apt to get sick (with both HIV and other diseases), which then in turn feeds into the other problems discussed here.

> **Sub-Saharan African Countries with High Prevalence of HIV/AIDS**
>
> *(information from UNAIDS: World AIDS Day 2012 Report)*
>
> | Nation | Individuals with HIV/AIDS |
> |---|---|
> | South Africa | 5.6 million |
> | Nigeria | 3 million |
> | United Republic of Tanzania | 1.6 million |
> | Kenya | 1.6 million |
> | Uganda | 1.4 million |
> | Mozambique | 1.4 million |
> | Zimbabwe | 1.2 million |
> | Zambia | 970,000 |
> | Ethiopia | 790,000 |

> **Did You Know?**
>
> *In the United States, AIDS is the third leading cause of death among black women ages 34 to 44.*

Family Structure

As people get sick and die, the structures of many families change. Deaths of adult men tend to have a larger impact on household income, while a woman's death has especially severe consequences for children because in most societies, including European and North American, women are the main caregivers. More and more households are headed by grandparents or by women without husbands.

In many African countries, fostering orphans is a common cultural practice; if your aunt and uncle died, for example, or your mother's best friend, your parents would take your cousins or the friend's children

Why HIV Testing is Important for Adolescents

Adolescents engage in behaviors that put them at risk for HIV infection. Among U.S. high school students surveyed in 2011:

- 47 percent have had sexual intercourse at least once.

- 40 percent of currently sexually active students did not use a condom the last time they had sex.

- 15 percent have had four or more sex partners.

- 6 percent had sexual intercourse for the first time before age 13.

- 2 percent have injected illegal drugs at least once.

Many young people are already infected, and the numbers are growing.

- Approximately 68,600 young people ages 13–24 years were living with HIV infection at the end of 2008; of those, nearly 60 percent did not know they were infected.

- In 2009, an estimated 8,300 young people aged 13–24 years were newly diagnosed with HIV infection.

- Although overall rates of HIV diagnoses remained stable from 2006 to 2009, HIV diagnosis rates increased for youth aged 15–19 and 20–24 years over the same period.

- HIV infection rates remain disproportionately high among black and Hispanic adolescents and are still increasing among young men who have sex with men.

(the above information was taken from the CDC website: www.cdc.gov/healthyyouth/sexualbehaviors/pdf/hivtesting_adolescents.pdf)

into your family. In areas where AIDS is so prevalent, though, the rapid rise in the number of orphans may overwhelm the traditional support system of extended families. Many of the households that take in orphans are already poor, and the extra mouths to feed are significant financial burdens.

AIDS has left many women widows in Africa and other developing regions. Traditionally, remarriage is one way many societies deal with the economic and emotional losses of widowhood. Especially in developing nations, women may have few work opportunities that would allow them to support themselves and their children, and so remarriage is not only expected but also necessary. In parts of Africa, widows are "inherited" by the

> **Did You Know?**
>
> In most African societies, women cannot inherit their husband's property. This means that when their husbands die, if they do not remarry, they are more likely to move back to live with their own kin.

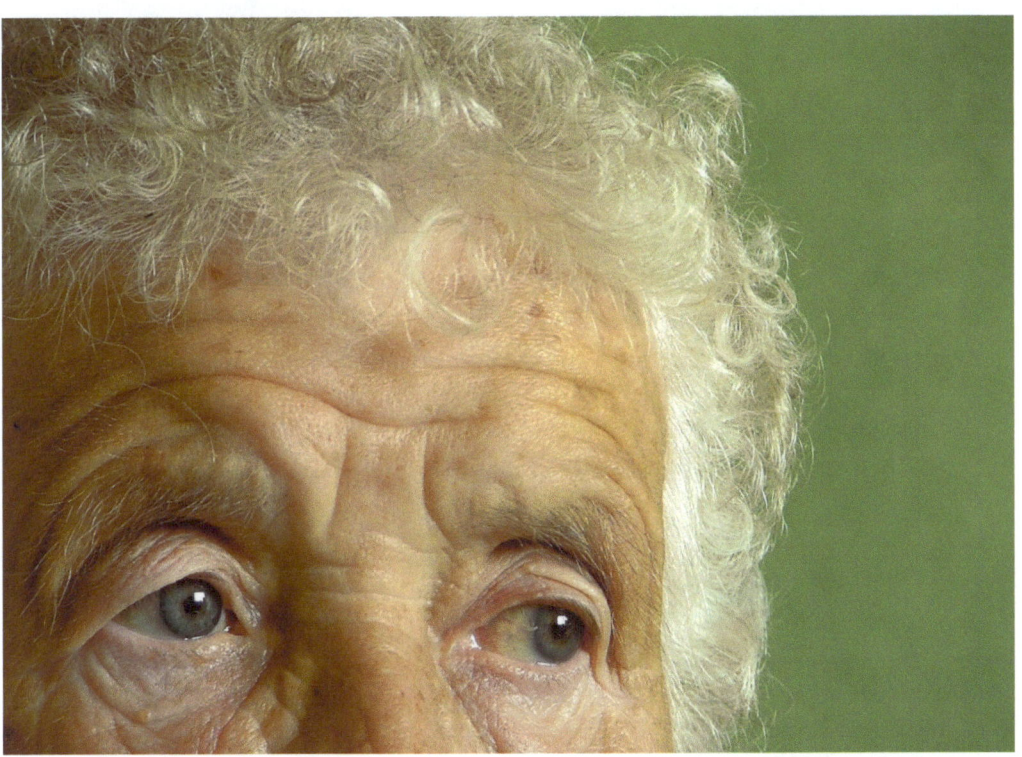

AIDS places a heavy burden on many older people, who are forced to become the caregivers for grandchildren at a time in their life when they have less money and less energy.

Real People

Achariya is a 77-year-old woman who lives in Cambodia with her six grandchildren. Their parents died of AIDS several years ago, and now she struggles to take care of them. Meanwhile, Achariya faces a variety of health concerns of her own. She says, "When I was young, I worked hard to feed my family. I thought that when I got old, they would take care of me. But now my sons are all dead, and I am left to care for their children. I have rheumatism, and it's very difficult for me to walk or stand. I sold my rice field to buy medicines for my sons before they died, and now I no longer have money to buy food and medicine for the children and me. I have to work in other people's fields, and I am in constant pain. But nobody takes care of me. There is no one left to take care of me."

husband's brother or another male relative, and through that union, she and her children continue to have access to property and other means of support. However, when a husband dies from AIDS, the wife is likely to be infected too, and remarriage poses a risk of spreading the disease. If the woman looks sick, she may be left with no means of support; however, if she appears to be healthy (regardless of the fact that she may be infected with HIV without knowing it), she often remarries and spreads the virus to another man.

AIDS adds stress to the lives of older persons when it kills their adult children, who would otherwise have been responsible for their care. When their children die, leaving behind children of their own, older people must take on the role of caregivers for their orphaned grandchildren. This means they will need more money for their household at a time in their lives when they have less income and less

Did You Know?

In 2009, AIDS was the sixth leading cause of death of 25- to 44-year-olds in the United States.

ability to work. This problem is seen among black Americans as well as Africans.

Education

When parents get sick, children in many societies leave school to care for them and for younger brothers and sisters. In some societies, children must get jobs or do farm work to help support the family. When both parents die, children are much less likely than other children to be in school; based on a recent survey in the United Republic of Tanzania, only 52 percent of children who lost both parents attended school, compared to 71 percent of those with who had at least one biological parent in the household. Another study in Uganda found that attendance declined 26 percent in older children whose parents had HIV/AIDS.

Migration

With so many members of society unable to function and do their jobs in both the home and the workplace, many people move away from their original communities. Sometimes entire households

Children living in households where a family member has AIDS may stay home from school to care for younger siblings.

disband, with members scattering to various other communities. A study in rural South Africa, for example, found that households in which an adult had died due to AIDS were nearly four times as likely to dissolve as other households.

The Societal Cost of HIV/AIDS

The *economic* cost of the AIDS pandemic is immense. In the United States, for example, HIV treatment can cost $15,000 per patient per year. This treatment slows the progress of the disease, but it does not eliminate HIV; the drugs must be taken regularly from the time of diagnosis for the rest of the patient's life or the virus will bounce back, as dangerous and life-threatening as ever. This means that the cost of treatment over a person's lifetime can be enormous.

Meanwhile, in most developing nations, societies cannot afford to treat their HIV-infected citizens with these drugs. For instance, in 2013, the United States had an average government spending of $8,233 per year per person for medical care, while Uganda's government had a spending of $30 per person each year. But when nations like Uganda cannot pay for treatment, it passes along other medical

Many people in Africa migrate from region to region as a result of AIDS' impact. In doing so, communities are broken, and people lose their old support systems.

costs to the society. If people cannot get the proper treatment for HIV/AIDS, they will likely become sick and fill hospital beds more often.

Societies around the world are paying a staggering cost because of HIV/AIDS. The virus has killed millions of adults, many of whom have left orphaned children who then need society's care. Many others have left surviving spouses who also are ill, need treatment, and cannot work. Families cannot find money to pay for funerals, and employers must find and train new employees. This problem is eating away at developing nations' economies. According to an article in the *Los Angeles Times*, "The epidemic's direct and indirect consequences are wiping out the gains that many of these countries have made in the past 30 years." Meanwhile, the disease also has steep financial costs in developed nations.

HIV/AIDS is not only a disease that affects individuals. It is society's disease—and together, the world's societies must find a way to combat it.

Ask the Doctor

My mother says the government should pay for medicines to treat poor people with AIDS, but my dad thinks that it's not fair that our taxes be raised because of something that's not our fault. I'm confused. Which one is right?

Your mom and dad sound like they're expressing two important viewpoints on society. Some people believe that it's the government's job to take care of its people; the money to do this comes from taxes. This approach is often called socialism. Other people believe that churches, charities, businesses, and private individuals should take care of these needs and that governments should stay out of such concerns. This philosophy, often called capitalism, is based on the idea that if government leaves businesses alone, the economy will grow, which in turn will be better for all the people in the society. You will have to decide which viewpoint makes most sense to you. However, in the case of HIV/AIDS treatment, someone needs to make treatment affordable (whether it's the government that takes action or private businesses), because ultimately the cost of so many sick people in a society is far greater than the cost of treatment. In other words, from a purely economic perspective (leaving what's "right" and "wrong" out of it), it would be cheaper to spend money preventing and treating HIV/AIDS than it is paying for the cost to businesses and the economy in lost wages, lost employees, and lost educational opportunities.

STRAIGHT FROM THE SOURCE

(From UNDP issues paper #30.)

The Impact of HIV/AIDS on Children

Children are affected by HIV/AIDS in ways that can diminish their childhoods and as a result limit choices and opportunities for successful survival throughout their lives. Circumstances of an individual's life and their social context in family and community during childhood can increase the probability they will one day be exposed to, and infected by, HIV. In order to develop appropriate means of enabling and protecting people, either as children or as adults, against infection and the effects of HIV/AIDS, adequate and judicious attention needs to be given to the rights and realities of childhood.

HIV and AIDS are brutal escalators of other cruelties which children endure. In today's world the majority of people living in poverty are women and children. Three quarters of the 24,000 daily deaths (more than 8 million every year) related to hunger are among those under the age of five (The Hunger Project). One hundred and twenty million children between the ages of 5 and 14 work in conditions that are hazardous to healthy growth and development (ILO). Estimates suggest that as many as 100 million children worldwide are homeless or spend most of their time surviving on the streets (UNICEF). Massive populations of families with children are displaced and often separated because of conflict and natural disasters. According to the United Nations Expert Report on the Impact of Armed Conflict on Children, prepared by Graça Machel, more than half of the near 60 million people displaced by war are children with millions separated from their families. Millions more have been injured, disabled, orphaned and died in armed conflict. Children are used as soldiers and forced to kill; raped by soldiers or made to watch their mothers and sisters raped and their families murdered. Added to these, children are victimised and trafficked as commodities for sale in local and global sexual prostitution and pornography industries. Estimates are that at any time, as many as one million children are involved in the commercial sexual exploitation arena every day. (ECPAT, World Congress Against Commercial Sexual Exploitation of Children). Countless others are physically, sexually and psychologically abused in what should be the secure confines of their homes and neighborhoods.

The roles that children fill as poor, hungry, exploited and abused human beings increase their vulnerability to HIV infection. This can occur directly through those activities known to be associated with transmission, or indirectly as occurs when earlier harm turns children into vulnerable adults. For example those with a history of childhood physical or sexual abuse have also been found in adolescence or adulthood to be more likely than non-abused peers to engage in behaviors that place them at high risk of HIV infection.

What Do You Think?

- According to this article, why are children particularly vulnerable to HIV?

- What are the "rights and realities" of childhood?

- Why do you think it's important that a society take care of its children?

Find Out More

To learn more about the cost of HIV/AIDS on society, check out these websites:

Thirty Years of HIV/AIDS: Snapshots of an Epidemic
www.amfar.org/thirty-years-of-hiv/aids-snapshots-of-an-epidemic

Counting the Cost of AIDS
www.economist.com/node/671525

World Bank: HIV/AIDS
web.worldbank.org

Here's what you need to know

- How are societies working to fight AIDS around the world?
- What are private business doing to help fight HIV/AIDS?
- What changes are developed nations making to fight the spread of HIV/AIDS? How has the black community in particular helped?
- What has Brazil done to fight HIV/AIDS? Why might this not work in other countries?
- What organizations work to fight HIV/AIDS internationally?
- What are nongovernmental organizations? How are they helping? What can they do that governments cannot?
- How can an individual help to change a society?

Words to Understand

Apartheid is an official policy that separates blacks from whites.

Controversial means that people do not agree on an issue.

Priority means that something has the highest level of importance.

Pharmaceutical has to do with medicinal drugs.

Activism is when people take a public and vocal stand to bring about change in reference to a particular issue.

Disparities are differences between two groups.

Abstinence means not having sex at all.

Mortality refers to death.

Patents are legal grants that confer upon the creator of an invention the sole right to make, use, and sell that invention for a set period of time.

A person who is *conservative* is resistant to changes in society.

Advocacy means speaking up on behalf of an individual or a group of people.

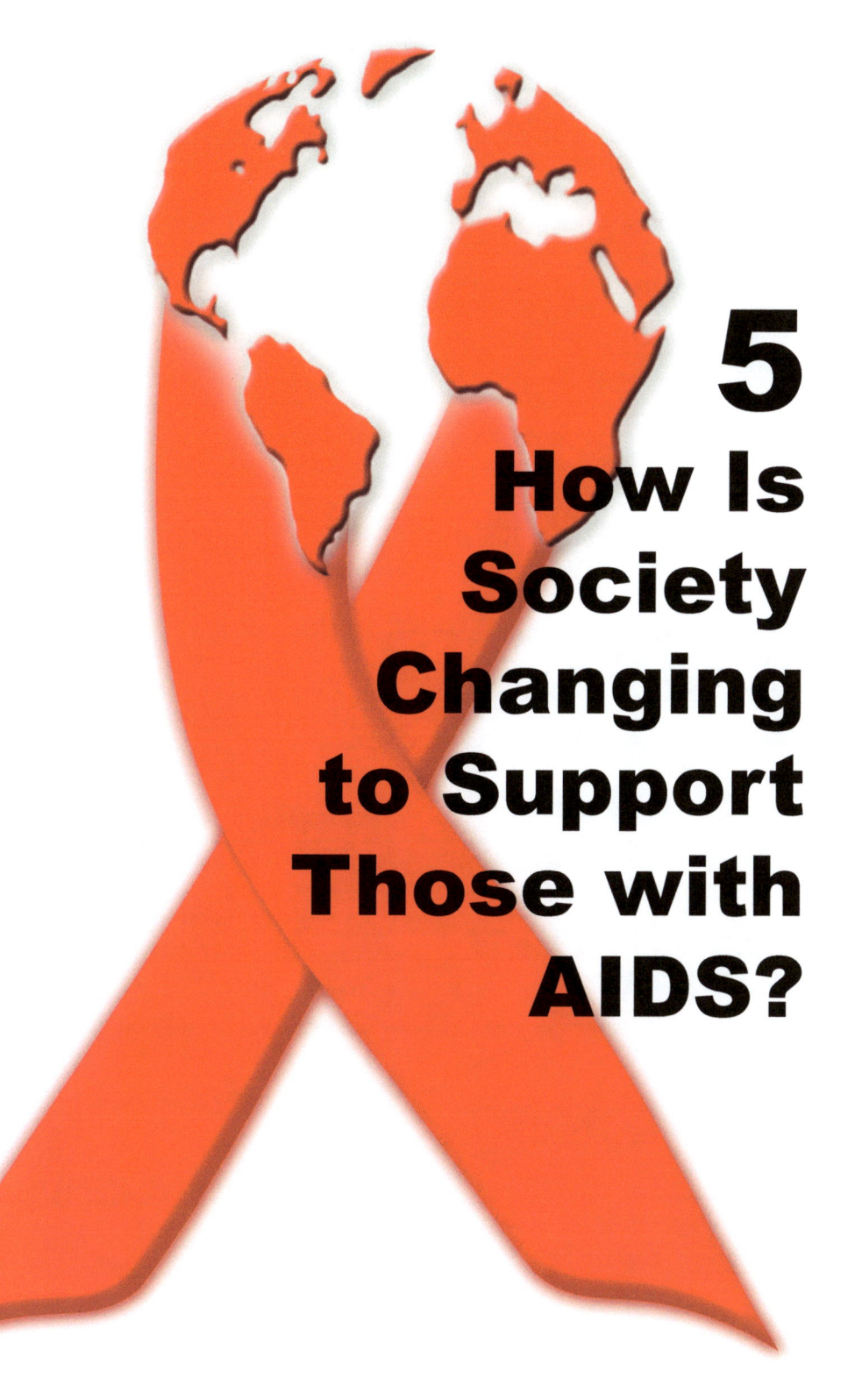

5
How Is Society Changing to Support Those with AIDS?

how do AIDS & society connect?

Did You Know?

President Obama requested an HIV/AIDS budget of $29.7 billion for 2014. This will be split so that $23.5 billion will be used domestically, and $6.2 billion will contribute to combat HIV/AIDS globally.

Since the introduction of the first life-prolonging treatments for AIDS in 1987, many people in developed nations, even among the poor, took the drugs and often lived longer than they would have otherwise. Meanwhile, if you got HIV/AIDS and lived in a developing country, unless you were very rich or very lucky, you would probably not get the medicines you needed—and you would die. Some people have called this "medical *apartheid*," a system that separates the world's poor, brown-skinned people from those with lighter skins and more opportunities. But things are beginning to change. Societies are make adjustments in important ways.

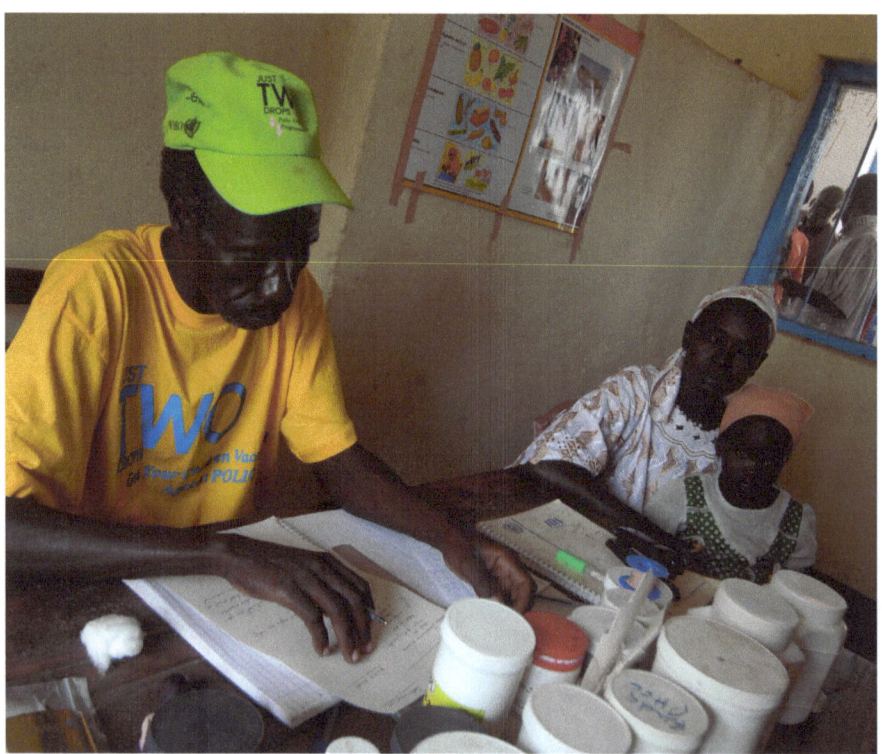

People in Africa and other developing nations have less access to health care. Here, for example, patients in the Sudan walk miles to come to this small clinic, where medicines and other supplies are limited.

Businesses

The idea of providing costly life-saving drugs and complex medical care to people with HIV/AIDS in developing countries was considered *controversial* by many governments, *humanitarian* organizations, and health-care professionals. With so many needs and crises in the world, not everyone believed that HIV/AIDS treatment should be a *priority*. After 20 years and millions of agonizing deaths from AIDS, mounting public pressure combined with the UN's efforts persuaded the *pharmaceutical* industry to reduce its prices by 80 to 90 percent for HIV medications. Botswana became the first African country to take advantage of these lower prices, and, according to the 2011 UNAIDS report, universal access to HIV/AIDS treatment (80 percent coverage or greater) has been achieved in this nation.

> **Did You Know?**
>
> Over 15,000 people died of AIDS in the United States in 2010 alone, yet AIDS is increasingly seen as an "overseas" or an "African" problem, rather than something that directly affects U.S. citizens. The PEPFAR program tends to receive greater attention and attract considerably more comment in the media than the work taking place to fight AIDS within the United States.

What Developed Nations Are Doing

The United States and other developed nations have increased their spending on HIV/AIDS in recent years, and social discrimination for those with HIV/AIDS has diminished. Various AIDS organizations have helped bring about the changes seen in developed nations. Vocal activism by groups such as ACT UP has helped make us more aware and concerned about those living with the virus. Activism also improved research into the illness, and resulted in a significant lowering of costs for many of the earliest HIV and AIDS drugs.

Unfortunately, the activism of the 1980s and early 1990s is harder to find in the twenty-first–century world. With the introduction of combination therapy in the mid-1990s, HIV moved from being a fatal to a chronic, controllable condition in many developed nations. As the drugs have improved, so has the outlook for people living with HIV. The general reduction in levels of hysteria and fear surrounding

72   how do AIDS & society connect?

> **Did You Know?**
>
> Needle exchange programs allow IV drug users to turn in dirty needles for clean ones. These programs are very controversial, however, as some people believe they condone drug use. In Australia, however, this practice is credited with nearly eliminating HIV transmission within the IV drug user community.

the illness has also meant less prejudice and ignorance for those living with the condition. This is a good thing on the one hand—but on the other hand, it has meant that AIDS has once more returned to being a comparatively overlooked illness.

Black Inequality

Black Americans pay a particularly heavy AIDS toll. According to black politician and minister Jesse Jackson, "AIDS has been allowed to stalk and murder Black America like a serial killer because we have been a compliant victim, submitting

Black women are one of American society's most at-risk populations.

through inaction. It is now time for us to fight AIDS like the major civil rights issue it is."

The American government counteracts these criticisms by saying that the U.S. Centers for Disease Control (CDC) actually devotes about half of its HIV budget to the black community, which they argue is a reasonable proportion given that African Americans make up half of all AIDS cases in total. The CDC currently funds several projects around the United States that address the epidemic in African Americans, including rapid HIV testing programs in traditionally black universities and colleges across the country, a variety of research programs targeted at the black community, and the Minority AIDS Initiative, which addresses health *disparities* and provides prevention programs to ethnic minority groups at high risk of HIV. The CDC also runs a variety of advertising campaigns, many of which target black churches (since around 80 percent of African Americans are believed to belong to a church). The CDC provided millions of dollars to facilitate HIV testing and improve early HIV diagnoses in areas with high levels of HIV within local black communities.

Political leaders are also changing their approach to HIV/AIDS. In his 2006 state of the Union address, President Bush acknowledged the important role of Christian institutions, and pledged to work more "closely with African American churches and faith-based groups, to deliver rapid HIV tests to millions, end the stigma of AIDS, and come closer to the day when there are no new infections in America."

Many African American churches have mobilized against AIDS. The Balm in Gilead is an example of an organization that works through black churches around the United States to stop the spread of HIV and provide support to those infected. Founder Pernessa C. Seele, founder of The Balm, acknowledged,

> There is no doubt that the link between HIV/AIDS, drug abuse and sexual activity has been a stumbling block for churches who feel that such behavior is contrary to their tenets.

> **Did You Know?**
> America's international spending on AIDS-related projects has increased substantially in recent years. The President's Emergency Fund for AIDS Relief (PEPFAR) was a program set up in 2003 by President George W. Bush to fight HIV/AIDS around the world. This program is still active today.

. . . Fortunately, increasing numbers of churches are realizing that providing AIDS education and social services is consistent with the teachings of Jesus Christ. Clearly, Jesus' actions on behalf of the sick show us how we should behave during this age of AIDS.

In June 2006, black politicians, clergy members, and community leaders signed a "Declaration of Commitment to End the AIDS Epidemic in Black America," in which they promised to do everything in their power to address the epidemic in their communities. At

Children growing up in poverty within the black American community are at greater risk for contracting HIV/AIDS.

a meeting in Toronto, Canada, eight high-profile African American organizations pledged to work together to reverse the spread of HIV in the black community, and to openly discuss homosexuality, drug use, and sex within prisons.

As a result of these changing trends in society, the overall number of infections among blacks in North America has been dropping. In the United States, this may be partly due to different needle exchange programs that have caused a massive decline in the number of injecting drug users being infected with HIV. However, HIV/AIDS in the African American community is still a serious problem, with almost 25,000 new infections occurring each year in the United States.

Education Programs

In 1996, the U.S. Congress made federal funding available for a five-year period to teach abstinence-only education in schools; meanwhile, federal funding for any other type of sex education was not made available. Between 1996 and 2009, more than $1.5 billion was spent funding abstinence education. Unfortunately, studies have shown that abstinence-only education is not very effective at slowing the spread of HIV among young adults. In his proposed 2014 fiscal year budget, President Obama eliminated funding for abstinence education in order to promote an educational program that focuses on contraception.

What Developing Nations Are Doing

Meanwhile, societies in developing nations are also working to make changes that will halt the progression of HIV. Brazil is one nation that has been very successful.

When AZT (one of the first effective drugs available to treat HIV) was first developed in the late 1980s, small quantities were made available for free in Brazil's São Paulo state. Then, in 1991, Brazil's government announced that the drug would be available for free to all Brazilians that needed it. In 1996, when another HIV drug was released, HAART, once again, the drugs were available for free. Brazil's AIDS *mortality* rate began to decline; by 2002, Brazil's Ministry of Health estimated that the availability of these medications had prevented around 358,000 HIV-related hospitalizations, resulting in a saving of more than US$1.1 billion.

> **What Do You Think?**
>
> *Big pharmaceutical companies like Merck argue that Brazil's policies are unfair to the patent holders and will discourage investment in AIDS drug research and production. The U.S.-Brazil Business Council called the move, "A major step backward for the country's development. Brazil is working to attract investment in innovative industries that rely on intellectual property, and this move will likely cause investments to go elsewhere."*

Brazil has served as an example to other nations. However, its actions are also considered controversial. The Brazilian government refuses to comply with **patents** on HIV medications, and other nations, including Thailand, have done the same. This means that in Brazil, cheaper, generic HIV drugs are given out, rather than the expensive patented drugs. Big U.S. pharmaceutical companies are not happy—but the Brazilian government stood firm, stating that the health of the people was the main priority.

The American government has also not approved of other Brazilian HIV-prevention policies. When working with developing countries, the U.S. government encourages them to adopt an "ABC" approach to HIV prevention: 1. Abstinence, 2. Being faithful to one partner, 3. Condom use. Brazil, however, places a heavier emphasis on condom use and refuses to stick to an ABC approach. On top of this, Brazilian society is fighting HIV among its sex workers—and the United States refuses aid to any HIV/AIDS prevention schemes that don't directly oppose the sex trade. In 2005, the Brazilian government refused the U.S. government's offer of $40 million funding for HIV and AIDS programs, because it would have required them to state that they are against the practice of commercial sex work. Katia Guimaraes from Brazil's National AIDS program stated, "Prostitutes are very major partners in this program. They work along with us. We could never say that we are against prostitution, because it is not illegal in Brazil. It's a tolerated, regulated profession." In June of 2013 though, the United States's anti-prostitution pledge was struck down, opening up the possibility of America helping to fund some of Brazil's HIV and AIDS programs.

Meanwhile, Brazilian society uses a variety of techniques to fight HIV. Free condoms are handed out at public events such as carnivals;

How Is Society Changing to Support Those with AIDS? 77

in 2011, at in Rio de Janeiro, 89 million free condoms were distributed. Non-government organizations (NGOs) working in Brazil's shanty towns educated young people about AIDS and encourage them to act as "information spreaders," passing the word on to their peers. HIV prevention messages are also promoted through a variety

Carnival in Brazil is a time when sexuality is celebrated. The HIV/AIDS programs in Brazil work within this societal framework to promote safer sex practices.

> ## What Can the World Learn from Brazil?
>
> Many developing countries have adopted Brazil's guidelines for treatment and prevention of HIV, and the World Health Organization asked the chief of Brazil's National AIDS Program to visit Geneva to help formulate new policies for fighting AIDS around the world. Of course, not all of Brazil's program will work in all societies, but some major elements could possibly be encouraged in other societies to fight HIV/AIDS:
>
> - a strong relationship between the government, civil society groups, and NGOs
>
> - strong political leadership and commitment to fight the epidemic
>
> - a tolerant, nonjudgmental approach to HIV prevention
>
> - a strong focus on condom promotion
>
> - the provision of free treatment to all, and aggressive efforts to minimize the cost of medication
>
> - a commitment to fighting stigma and discrimination, and encouraging a culture where people living with HIV are not looked down upon, but are actively involved in helping the government respond to the epidemic

of media, including television, newspapers, and public spaces such as billboards and bus shelters. The messages conveyed by these campaigns are among the most explicit that any government has put forward, which also causes controversy among some **conservative** groups. Brazilian celebrities have helped to get these messages across; in one media campaign, the Brazilian pop-singer Kelly Key tells her teenage audience, "Show how you've grown up. This carnival, use condoms." Telenovelas (television soap operas), which are very popular in Brazil, feature characters living with HIV and demonstrate prevention and treatment techniques.

The United Nations

In September 2000, 189 of the world's nations met for the Millennium Summit. There the leaders agreed to work together to reduce poverty and improve lives. An important goal as part of this was to

How Is Society Changing to Support Those with AIDS? 79

fight AIDS. A year after the Millennium Summit, in June 2001, heads of state and representatives of governments met at a United Nations General Assembly Special Session dedicated to HIV/AIDS. The meeting was a milestone in the battle against AIDS because it made a public statement to the entire world that the AIDS epidemic has caused untold suffering and death. The UN Special Session also encouraged the world to take hope: with effort and resources, communities and countries can change the epidemic's deadly course. At the meeting, the world's leaders issued the Declaration of Commitment on HIV/AIDS, intended to be a tool to guide and ensure the world's action, commitment, support, and resources in the battle against AIDS.

Kelly Key is a Brazilian teen idol who has used her voice to promote HIV/AIDS education.

80   how do AIDS & society connect?

As a result, the Joint United Nations Programme on HIV and AIDS (UNAIDS) was formed to spearhead the global action against the epidemic. UNAIDS' mission includes:

- preventing the transmission of HIV
- providing care and support to those already living with the virus
- reducing the vulnerability of individuals and communities to HIV
- alleviating the impact of the epidemic

UNAIDS works with businesses, charities, other non-governmental agencies (NGOs), and private citizens to unite and coordinate many kinds of efforts to achieve the "Millennium Promise."

The United Nations headquarters in New York City is a meeting place for the world's leaders to discuss the problem of AIDS in the world's societies.

Real People

Author Kay Warren wrote an article for CNN, where she described a woman with AIDS she had met in Africa:

When I met her, this emaciated woman was homeless, living under a tree. She had unrelenting diarrhea, little food, no earthly possessions, and only an elderly auntie who had taken pity on her to care for her needs.... The African pastors who brought me to visit her told me that she had been evicted from her village when it became known that she had AIDS. Now, in this second village, her tiny stick house had mysteriously burned after her status became known. A short time later, Joana died—rejected, abandoned, persecuted and destitute.

We may think this doesn't happen in the United States. "People who are HIV-positive are treated better than that here," we say. But I'm not so sure. I live in affluent Orange County, California, yet a disabled man in my area who was HIV positive was not allowed to enter his brother's home. He and his wife could live in the backyard, but he couldn't come inside. To bathe him, his wife had to attach a nozzle to a hose and shoot him with a hard spray of water that would hopefully dislodge dirt and grime. The family dog was treated better than this man; at least it could go in the house.

Horrific and startling images confront each of us. ... You can do what I did for years—choose to ignore it all because it was too painful—or you can become disturbed—seriously, dangerously disturbed—so disturbed that you are compelled to do something.

> **The Eight Millennium Development Goals of the United Nations**
>
> 1. Eradicate extreme poverty and hunger.
> 2. Achieve universal primary education.
> 3. Promote gender equality and empower women.
> 4. Reduce child mortality.
> 5. Improve maternal health.
> 6. Combat HIV/AIDS, malaria, and other diseases.
> 7. Ensure environmental sustainability.
> 8. Develop a global partnership for development.

NGOs

NGOs—non-governmental organizations—are people who want to change society who have joined together to form an organization. They're ordinary people who believe so strongly in a particular cause that they get organized, get funding (usually from donations), and get to work. These organizations have become more and more influential in the battle against AIDS. They bring about change in our society.

People Making a Difference

People all over the world are joining the fight to end AIDS and poverty. Most of them have names you've probably never heard—but many of them are famous people who use their position to bring more attention to the cause they've taken on. From hip-hop artists to fashion models, movie stars to talk show hosts, more and more members of our society are getting involved.

One of the stars who's leading the battle is Bono from the rock group U2. In October 2006, he joined with talk show

> **Did You Know?**
>
> *NGOs became a powerful force in the nineteenth century. They helped end slavery and were the driving force behind women's right to vote.*

How Is Society Changing to Support Those with AIDS? 83

NGOs bring medical aid to remote African communities.

host Oprah Winfrey to promote a line of clothing and accessories called (PROJECT) RED. Portions of the sales from these products go to the Global Fund, an organization that fights AIDS, tuberculosis, and malaria. Bono explained, "Now you're buying jeans and T-shirts, and you're paying for 10 women in Africa to get medication for their children with HIV."

Oprah Winfrey has used her celebrity status to advance the fight against AIDS.

How Is Society Changing to Support Those with AIDS?

Bono is one of the celebrities who is working hard to battle AIDS, especially in Africa.

Bono was also involved in the Live 8 concert on July 2, 2005, an attempt to pressure the G8—leaders of the world's powerful nations—to forgive debts and increase aid for poorer countries. Bono said about the concert, "We are not looking for charity, we are looking for justice." More than a thousand musicians performed on ten

Using Debt Relief to Fight AIDS & Poverty

When the world's developed nations forgive the debts of poorer nations, it frees up money that can be used to fight AIDS and poverty. Here is what some of the world's poor nations have done with the money they gained from help with their debts.

Country	AIDS-Related Actions
Benin	Increased budget for improved health for pregnant mothers and for HIV/AIDS. Government created comprehensive HIV/AIDS strategy.
Cameroon	Curbed infection rates through increased use of condoms by port workers, truckers, soldiers, and commercial sex workers. Expanded HIV testing and counseling services. Introduced AIDS education in secondary schools.
Guinea-Bissau	Adopted strategic framework to fight HIV/AIDS. Informed high-risk population (ages 14–29) of transmission and prevention methods.
Malawi	Established fully staffed National AIDS Control Secretariat. Ensured that 75 percent of all condom outlet points are stocked with condoms. Made testing kits available at all blood transfusion sites. Implemented behavior change communication strategy. Managed sexually transmitted infections in all hospitals.
Mauritania	Maintained HIV prevalence rate at the 1998 level of less than 1.2 percent maximum of blood donors.
Mozambique	Implemented the National Multisectoral Plan on HIV/AIDS.
Rwanda	Adopted new strategy and action plan for HIV/AIDS control.
Tanzania	Implemented national spearhead campaign against HIV/AIDS, including visits to 75 percent of all districts.
Zambia	Created a fully staffed National HIV/AIDS Council secretariat. Introduced AIDS awareness and prevention programs in at least 10 government ministries.

Source: World Bank website on HIPC, web.worldbank.org/WBSITE/EXTERNAL/TOPICS/EXTDEBTDEPT/0,,contentMDK:20260411~menuPK:64166739~pagePK:64166689~piPK:64166646~theSitePK:469043,00.html

stages around the world, broadcast on almost two hundred stations as millions watched. Almost all the top popular music artists of the world were involved, including the Who, Pink Floyd, Madonna, Mariah Carey, Kanye West, REM, Shakira, Coldplay, Brian Wilson, and U2. Bono and Paul McCartney opened the London show together. Five days after the Live 8 event, world leaders pledged to double aid to Africa from $25 to $50 billion.

Society is made up individuals, and each individual—even if the rest of the world has never heard that person's name—has the power to shape the direction society goes. Problems as big as AIDS and poverty need big solutions. They can only be solved when our entire international society—governments, superstars, organizations, and ordinary people like you—all work together.

Ask the Doctor

I've heard that antiretroviral treatment can cure AIDS. Is that true—and what is it?

Unfortunately, there is no cure for HIV/AIDS. But medicines that fght HIV have helped many people with HIV and AIDS live years and even decades longer than was possible in the past. Antiretroviral medications fight the virus that causes AIDS; although they cannot completely kill all the virus a person might have, these medications keep it from reproducing as quickly. As HIV reproduces itself, variations of the virus emerge, including some that are resistant to antiretroviral drugs. This is why doctors recommend that people infected with HIV take a combination of antiretroviral drugs known as highly active antiretroviral therapy, or HAART. This strategy, which typically combines drugs from at least two different classes of antiretroviral drugs, has been shown to effectively suppress the virus when used properly. The person is not cured—and he or she can still pass HIV onto someone else—but he or she is much more likely to be able to live longer in good health, sometimes for many years.

STRAIGHT FROM THE SOURCE

(From BlackAids, October 25, 2007, www.blackaids.org)

Black Ministers Taking the Lead

Black faith leaders from around the country convened earlier this month to plot a legislative strategy for ending the AIDS epidemic in Black America. The remarkable meeting—which drew roughly 200 participants, including not only African American clergy but also Black medical professionals and congressional members—was a critical step in a clergy-led campaign to push both local and national elected officials into action. . . .

The ministers drafted a statement of priorities in which they vowed to push HIV testing, treatment and overall AIDS awareness in their own congregations, and then called on lawmakers to draft and pass a National HIV/AIDS Elimination Act. The clergy statement added to a chorus of calls for the federal government to develop an overarching national plan to deal with the epidemic. After 26 years, the U.S. still has no overall strategy guiding its response to the domestic epidemic. The U.S. insists any nation receiving foreign assistance for an AIDS program have just that sort of plan and it is long past time that we have one of our own.

"The Act will include measurable goals, timetables, and specific objectives designed to eliminate the HIV/AIDS epidemic," the statement reads. "As a part of the National AIDS Plan, the Elimination Act will highlight and address the key structural drivers of the AIDS epidemic like poverty, low-literacy, stigma, unemployment, incarceration, racial disparities, and other structural drivers of the epidemic in the United States."

What Do You Think?

- This document indicates that literacy (the ability to read), unemployment, and incarceration all play a roll in making a society at risk for HIV/AIDS. How do you think these elements influence the transmission of HIV?

- Do you agree that churches need to be involved in issues like AIDS? Why or why not?

Find Out More

To find out more about what the world is doing to fight AIDS, check out these websites:

End Poverty by 2015
www.endpoverty2015.org

The United Nations: AIDS
www.un.org/en/globalissues/aids/index.shtml

NGOs International HIV/AIDS Alliance
www.aidsalliance.org/includes/Publication/cat0704_Capacity_analysis_toolkit_eng.pdf

For More Information on HIV/AIDS

Books

Flanagan, Wendy. *I Am HIV-Positive*. Portsmouth, N.H.: Heinemann, 2003.

Gallant, Joel. *100 Questions and Answers About HIV and AIDS*. New York: Jones & Bartlett, 2007.

Hinds, Maurene J. *Fighting the AIDS and HIV Epidemic: A Global Battle*. Berkeley Heights, N.J.: Enslow, 2007.

McFarlane, Katerine. *AIDS: Perspectives*. New York: Greenhaven, 2007.

McIntosh, Kenneth and Ida Walker. *Living with the Diagnosis: Youth with HIV/AIDS*. Philadelphia: Mason Crest, 2008.

Stine, Gerald. *AIDS Update 2008*. New York: McGraw-Hill, 2008.

Wagner, Viqi. *AIDS: Opposing Viewpoints*. New York: Greenhaven, 2007.

Whiteside, Alan. *HIV/AIDS: A Very Short Introduction*. New York: Oxford University Press, 2008.

Websites

AEGiS (AIDS Educational Global Information System)
www.aegis.org/en

AIDS Info from the U.S. Department of Health and Human Services
www.aidsinfo.nih.gov

AIDSMAP
www.aidsmap.com

For More Information on HIV/AIDS

AVERT
www.avert.org/aids.htm

The Body: The Complete HIV/AIDS Resource
www.thebody.com

CDC HIV/AIDS Factsheets
www.cdc.gov/hiv/resources/factsheets

HIV InSite (online textbook from the University of California)
hivinsite.ucsf.edu/InSite

Kaiser Family Foundation Daily HIV/AIDS Report
www.kff.org/hivaids

Kids' Health: HIV and AIDS
www.kidshealth.com/teen/sexual_health/stds/std_hiv.html

Mayo Clinic HIV/AIDS
www.mayoclinic.com/health/hiv-aids/DS00005

Medical News Today: HIV & AIDS
www.medicalnewstoday.com/sections/hiv-aids

MedlinePlus
www.nlm.nih.gov/medlineplus

United Nations Development Programme on HIV/AIDS
www.undp.org/content/undp/en/home/ourwork/hiv-aids/overview.html

WHO and AIDS
www.who.int/hiv/en

Glossary of HIV/AIDS–Related Terms

When you're reading about HIV/AIDS—or if someone you know has this disease—you may encounter lots of unfamiliar medical terms. This glossary can help you better understand this complicated disease and its treatments.

Acquired Immunity
The body's ability to fight a specific infection, which can be acquired by having and recovering from an infection, by being vaccinated against an infection, or by receiving antibodies through breast milk.

Acquired Immunodeficiency Syndrome (AIDS)
A disease of the body's immune system caused by HIV (human immunodeficiency virus) that leaves the body vulnerable to life-threatening conditions such as infections and cancer.

Acute HIV Infection
The period of rapid growth of the virus during the two to four weeks after HIV infection. Some (but not all) people will experience flu-like symptoms during this period, which can include fever, sore throat, inflamed lymph nodes, and a rash, lasting from a few days to a few weeks.

AIDS-Defining Condition
Any of a list of 29 illnesses that lead to a diagnosis of AIDS when occurring in a person with HIV. Included in the list are Kaposi's sarcoma, pneumocystis, recurrent pneumonia, pulmonary tuberculosis, invasive cervical cancer, and wasting syndrome.

AIDS-Related Cancer
One of the several cancers that are more common or more aggressive in people with HIV, including lymphomas, Kaposi's sarcoma, and cancers that affect the anus and the cervix.

AIDS-Related Complex
A group of conditions that often occur during the early stage of HIV infection, which can include recurrent fevers, unexplained weight loss, diarrhea, herpes, swollen lymph nodes, or fungal infection in the mouth and throat.

Antibody
Also known as immunoglobulin, a protein produced by the body's immune system that recognizes and fights germs and other foreign substances that enter the body.

Antigen
Anything that stimulates the body to produce antibodies to fight it, including bacteria, viruses, and pollen.

Antiretroviral
A medicine that interferes with the ability of a retrovirus (such as HIV) to make more copies of itself.

B-Cell Lymphoma
A type of cancer in the lymphatic tissue, to which people with HIV are more prone.

B Lymphocytes
Also known as B cells, these infection-fighting white blood cells develop in the bone marrow and spleen; in people with HIV, B lymphocytes' ability to do their job is damaged.

Branched Chain DNA Assay (bDNA Assay)
A test that measures a person's viral load (level of HIV present in the blood) to diagnose HIV and monitor disease progression, as well as treatment effectiveness.

Candidiasis
An infection caused by a yeast-like fungus that produces white patches on the skin, nails, and mucus membranes. It is considered an AIDS-defining condition in people with HIV.

Cardiomyopathy
A condition that weakens the heart muscle, which can cause irregular heartbeat and decreased heart function. It may occur in people with HIV.

CD4 Cell
Also known as helper T cell, these infection-fighting white blood

cells signal the other cells in the immune system to do their jobs. The number of CD4 cells in a blood sample indicates how healthy the person's immune system is. HIV infects and kills CD4 cells.

CD4 Cell Count
Measuring the number of CD4 cells in a blood sample is one of the most useful ways to tell how far HIV/AIDS has progressed. Healthcare providers use this count to determine when to begin or stop therapies and to measure response to treatments. A normal CD4 cell count is between 500 and 1,400 cells per cubic millimeter of blood. When an individual with HIV has a CD4 cell count at or below 200, he is considered to have AIDS.

CD8 Cell
Also called killer T cell, this is a type of white blood cell that is able to recognize and kill cells that are infected by a foreign invader.

Cervical Cancer
A condition in which a cancerous growth forms on the lower portion of the uterus, which is called the cervix; it is a type of cancer to which people with HIV/AIDS are more susceptible.

CIPRA (Comprehensive International Program on Research on AIDS)
A program run by the U.S. NIAID (National Institute on Allergy and Infectious Diseases) to support research and affordable treatment of HIV/AIDS in poor countries.

CMV (cytomegalovirus)
An infectious eye disease that is the most common cause of blindness in people with HIV.

Co-Infection
Infection with more than one germ at a time; for example, a person with HIV may also be infected with hepatitis C or tuberculosis (TB).

Combination Therapy
When two or more drugs are used together to treat HIV, which has proven to be more effective than using a single drug.

Glossary of HIV/AIDS–Related Terms

Contagious
When a disease passes easily between people through normal day-to-day contact. HIV is not contagious.

Cryptoccosis
An infection caused by a fungus that enters the body through the lungs and usually spreads to the brain. It is considered an AIDS-defining condition in people with HIV.

DNA (deoxyribonucleic acid)
Chemical structure that contains the genetic instructions for reproduction within all cells.

ELISA (enzyme-linked immunosorbent assay)
A sensitive laboratory test used to determine the presence of antibodies to HIV in the blood or saliva. Positive ELISA results should always be confirmed with another test called a Western blot.

End-Stage Disease
The final phase in the course of a disease that will lead to the person's death.

Entry Inhibitors
A class of anti-HIV drugs designed to interfere with HIV's ability to enter a host cell through the cell's surface.

Envelope
The outer protective membrane of HIV cells. Proteins in the envelope allow HIV to attach to and enter host cells.

Enzyme
A protein in the body that helps a chemical reaction happen.

Fusion Inhibitors
A class of anti-HIV drugs that gets in the way of HIV's outer envelope fusing with a host cell's membrane, thus preventing infection of the cell.

GART (genotypic antiretroviral resistance test) or Genotypic Assay
A test that determines if HIV is resistant to a particular drug. The test

HAART (highly active antiretroviral therapy)
Treatment regimens that aggressively suppress HIV from copying itself and thus slow the progression of HIV disease. It usually combines three or more anti-HIV drugs.

Helper T Cells
See *CD4 Cell*

Hemophilia
A hereditary blood defect, occurring almost exclusively in males, characterized by delayed clotting, which can lead to uncontrolled bleeding, even after minor cuts. Because hemophiliacs often receive blood transfusions to treat injuries, they were exposed to HIV during the 1970s, before doctors realized that the blood supply was infected.

HIV (human immunodeficiency virus)
The virus that causes AIDS.

HIV-1
The type of HIV responsible for most of the HIV infections around the world.

HIV-2
A virus that is closely related to HIV-1, which also causes AIDS. Although the two viruses are very similar, immunodeficiency seems to develop more slowly and to be milder in people who have HIV-2. Most people who have HIV-2 live in West Africa. Drugs used to treat HIV-1 are not always effective against HIV-2.

Immune Response
The body's reaction to a foreign invader, such as a bacteria, virus, or fungus.

Immune System
The cells and organs in the body, including the thymus, spleen, lymph nodes, B and T cells, and antigen-presenting cells, whose job is to protect the body against foreign invaders.

Glossary of HIV/AIDS-Related Terms

Immunocompromised
Unable to mount a normal immune response because of a damaged immune system.

Immunodeficiency
Unable to produce normal amounts of antibodies and/or immune cells.

Immunoglobulin (IG)
See **Antibody**

Immunosuppression
Inability of the immune system to function normally (which can be caused by treatments such as chemotherapy or by certain diseases such as HIV).

Immunotherapy
Treatment to stimulate or restore the body's ability to fight off diseases.

Incubation Period
The time between when a germ enters the body and when the person develops symptoms.

Infectious
A disease that can spread from person to person.

Integrase
An HIV protein that inserts the virus' genetic information into the infected cell.

Integrase Inhibitors
A class of anti-HIV drugs that prevents the integrase protein from inserting genetic information into the host cell.

Integration
The process by which HIV integrase inserts the virus' genetic material into a host cell.

Interleukin-2 (IL-2)
A protein that helps regulate the immune system by increasing the production of certain disease-fighting white blood cells. HIV infection reduces IL-2 levels, but a man-made version of IL-2 is being researched as a way to treat people with HIV.

Interleukin-7 (IL-7)
Another protein that regulates the immune system by increasing the body's production of certain white blood cells. Man-made IL-7 is used to treat HIV because it makes HIV copy itself in infected cells that are resting, allowing anti-retroviral drugs to target HIV in those cells.

Investigational Drug
Also known as an experimental drug, these medicines' safety and effectiveness have not yet been thoroughly tested.

Kaposi's Sarcoma (KS)
A type of cancer caused by an overgrowth of blood vessels, causing pinkish-purple bumps or spots on the skin. These can also occur inside the body, especially in the intestines, lungs, and lymph nodes, and when this happens, the condition can become life-threatening. KS is considered an AIDS-defining condition. A virus called Kaposi's sarcoma herpesvirus (KSHV) or human herpesvirus 8 often accompanies Kaposi's sarcoma.

Killer T Cell
See *CD8 Cell*

Latency
The time during which an infection is present within the body without producing any noticeable symptoms. Latency may last for a few years with an HIV infection.

Lentivirus
In Latin, *lente* means "slow;" these are viruses that have a long latency period (like HIV).

Glossary of HIV/AIDS–Related Terms

Lesion
An area on the skin where the tissue is abnormal, such as a sore or an infected patch.

Leukocytosis
An abnormally high white blood cell count, a condition that usually occurs during an infection.

Leukopenia
A lower than normal white blood cell count.

Long-Term Nonprogressors
People who have been infected with HIV for at least 7 years with no symptoms, stable CD4 counts of 600 or more, and no HIV-related diseases.

Lymph
A clear, yellowish fluid that carries white blood cells (which fight disease) from the blood to body tissues.

Lymph Nodes
Small immune system organs that are located throughout the body, where lymph is filtered as it carries white blood cells back from the body tissues to the blood.

Lymphadenopathy Syndrome (LAS)
Swollen and sometimes sore lymph nodes caused by infections (such as HIV, the flu, or mononucleosis) or lymphoma (cancer of the lymph tissue).

Lymphocyte
A type of infection-fighting white blood cell found in the blood and lymph.

Lymphoid Interstitial Pneumonitis (LIP)
A hardening of the parts of the lung that absorb oxygen for which there is no clear treatment. LIP is an AIDS-defining condition in children with HIV.

Lymphokines
Chemical messengers secreted by white blood cells that affect the immune response.

Macrophage
A type of disease-fighting white blood cell that destroys invaders and helps other immune system cells to do their jobs.

Malabsorption Syndrome
When the intestines cannot adequately absorb nutrients. This is a condition that is associated with HIV and that can lead to loss of appetite, muscle pain, and weight loss.

Memory T Cells
A type of infection-fighting T cell that recognizes foreign invaders it has encountered before (either during an earlier infection or from a vaccination). Memory T cells do their jobs faster and more strongly the second time they see the invader.

Meningitis
Inflammation of the membranes around the brain or spinal cord, which can be caused by bacteria, fungus, or a viral infection like HIV.

Microbes
Living organisms that can only be seen through a microscope, including bacteria, protozoa, viruses, and fungi.

Microsporidiosis
An intestinal infection caused by a parasite that causes diarrhea and loss of weight and strength in people with HIV.

Molluscum Contagiosum
A disease of the skin and mucus membranes that causes white or flesh-colored bumps on the face, neck, hands, underarms, and genitals. A virus causes the condition, but in people with HIV, it usually gets worse with time and does not respond to treatment.

Mucocutaneous
Relating to the mucus membranes and the skin (the eyes, mouth, lips, vagina, and anus, for example).

Mutation
A change or adaptation that can be passed down to future generations. The virus that causes AIDS mutates, which means that an individual strain of HIV can adapt to infect different cell types or to resist certain anti-HIV drugs. Mutations can only occur when the virus is copying itself and not when anti-HIV drugs have suppressed the virus to the point where it is not detectable.

Mycobacterium Avium Complex (MAC)
A life-threatening infection caused by two bacteria found in soil and dust, which is extremely rare in people who do not have HIV. It is considered an AIDS-defining condition in people with HIV.

Myelosuppression
Decreased bone marrow function that means that fewer red blood cells, white blood cells, and platelets (the part of the blood that causes clotting) are produced. It is a side effect of some anti-HIV drugs.

Myopathy
A disease of muscle tissue that can be a side effect of some anti-HIV drugs; HIV itself can also cause it.

Natural Killer Cells (NK cells)
White blood cells that kill tumor cells and other cells infected with viruses or other foreign invaders.

Neuropathy
A disorder caused by damaged nerve cells, which can produce a range of symptoms from a tingly feeling in the toes and fingers to paralysis. Some anti-HIV drugs cause neuropathy, as does HIV itself in some cases.

Neutropenia
A lower than normal number of *neutrophils* in the blood, which can increase the chance of getting bacterial infections. It can be caused by HIV infection, but some anti-HIV drugs also cause it.

Neutrophil
A type of white blood cell that engulfs and kills invaders such as bacteria.

Non-Nucleoside Reverse Transcriptase Inhibitors (NNRTIs)
A kind of anti-HIV drug that binds to and disables the protein that HIV-1 needs to copy itself, bringing an end to HIV-1 multiplication.

Nucleoside
An early version of a nucleotide, the building block that contains DNA and RNA, which are the chemical structures that store the cell's genetic material. Nucleosides must be changed chemically before they can make DNA and RNA.

Nucleoside Analogue Reverse Transcriptase Inhibitor (nuke)
A kind of anti-HIV drug that provides a "bad" version of the building block necessary for HIV reproduction. When it's used instead of a normal nucleoside, reproduction of the virus is halted.

Nucleotide
A building block of the chemical structures (DNA and RNA) that stores genetic information within the cell.

Nucleotide Analogue Reverse Transcriptase Inhibitor (nuke)
A kind of anti-HIV drug that provides a "bad" version of a nucleotide, which halts HIV reproduction.

Nukes
See *Nucleoside Analogue Reverse Transcriptase Inhibitor* and *Nucleotide Analogue Reverse Transcriptase Inhibitor.*

Opportunistic Infections (OIs)
Illnesses that occur in people with weakened immune systems, including people with HIV/AIDS. Common OIs in people with AIDS include Pneumocystis carinii pneumonia, histoplasmosis, toxoplasmosis, cryptosporidiosis, and some types of cancers.

Oral Hairy Leukoplakia (OHL)
A white, hairy, or bumpy patch caused by the Epstein-Barr virus (a member of the herpesvirus family) that appears on the side of the tongue and inside the cheeks, mainly in people with weakened immune systems (including people with HIV).

Osteoporosis
Loss of bone mass, density, and strength, which is usually brought on by old age but can also occur as a result of HIV infection or as a side effect of some anti-HIV drugs.

p24
The protein that surrounds the HIV core where the genetic material is found.

Palliative Care
Medical care that offers no cure but helps reduce the suffering and discomfort caused by the disease's symptoms.

Pancytopenia
A lower than normal level of all types of blood cells, including red blood cells, white blood cells, and platelets.

Paresthesia
Burning, tingling, or pins-and-needles sensations that can be caused as part of neuropathy brought on by certain anti-HIV drugs.

Passive Immunotherapy
A treatment approach that transfers antibodies from one person to another to help the receiver fight infections. An example in HIV treatment is when plasma from healthy HIV-infected people (who have high CD4 counts and high levels of anti-HIV antibodies) is given to people with AIDS who have lost CD4 cells and can no longer make their own antibodies. This treatment has not been very successful with adults, but it is still sometimes used with children who have HIV.

Perinatal Transmission
When a mother with HIV gives her child the virus, either within the womb, during labor and delivery, or through breastfeeding.

Photosensitivity
When skin responds more quickly to sunlight and ultraviolet light, causing sunburns and skin cancer more easily. It can be a side effect of some drugs and can also be caused by HIV infection.

Pill Burden
The number of pills taken each day. A high pill burden may make the person less likely to follow the treatment she needs.

Plasma
The clear, liquid part of the blood in which red blood cells, white blood cells, platelets, nutrients, and wastes are suspended.

Pneumocystis Jiroveci Pneumonia (PCP)
A lung infection that occurs in people with weakened immune systems, including those with HIV, whose first symptoms are difficulty breathing, high fever, and a dry cough. It is considered an AIDS-defining condition in people with HIV.

Post-Exposure Prophylaxis (PEP)
Administration of anti-HIV drugs within 72 hours of a high-risk exposure (such as unprotected sex, needle sharing, or injury) to help prevent HIV infection.

Protease
An enzyme that breaks down proteins into smaller chunks.

Protease Inhibitors (PIs)
A kind of anti-HIV drug that prevents HIV from reproducing by disabling HIV protease.

Protease-Sparing Regimen
An anti-HIV drug regimen that does not include a PI.

Protozoa
Tiny, one-celled animals that cause diseases, especially in people with weakened immune systems (including those with HIV). AIDS-defining infections such as toxoplasmosis and cryptosporidiosis are caused by protozoa.

Pulmonary
Having to do with the lungs.

q.d.
Once a day dosing instructions.

Glossary of HIV/AIDS–Related Terms

q.i.d.
Four times a day dosing instructions.

R5-Tropic Virus
A strain of HIV, also called M-tropic virus.

Receptor
A protein on the surface of a cell that acts as a binding site for substances outside the cell (such as HIV).

Remission
The time during which symptoms diminish or disappear, although the person is still infected.

Retrovirus
A type of virus that stores its genetic information in a single-strand RNA molecule, then builds a double-strand DNA version using an enzyme called reverse transcriptase, which is then integrated into the host cell's own genetic material. HIV is a retrovirus.

Reverse Transcriptase (RT)
An enzyme found in HIV and other retroviruses that converts single-strand RNA into double-strand DNA.

RNA (ribonucleic acid)
The chemical structure that carries genetic instructions for some viruses.

Seborrheic Dermatitis
A skin condition common in people with HIV where the skin is covered with loose, greasy, or dry scales that are white or yellowish. It can occur on the scalp, eyelids, eyebrows, ears, lips, and along any skin folds.

Sepsis
A blood-borne infection, usually caused by bacteria, to which people with HIV are more prone.

Superinfection
A new infection on top of an existing infection, such as when a person

with HIV-1 becomes infected with a new strain of HIV. Superinfection makes treatment more challenging.

T Cell
A type of disease-fighting white blood cell, which includes CD4 and CD8 cells. The "T" stands for thymus, where T cells mature.

Therapeutic HIV Vaccine
A vaccine used to treat a person who is already infected with HIV to boost his immune response and better control the virus.

Thymus
An organ behind the breastbone in the chest where infection-fighting T cells develop.

t.i.d.
Three times a day dosing instructions.

Tolerability
How well a medicine can be tolerated—or endured—by a person taking it.

Tolerance
A decreased response to repeated doses of a drug.

Toxoplasmosis
An infection caused by a protozoa that is carried by cats and birds, and is also found in soil contaminated by cat feces and in pork. Toxoplasmosis is an AIDS-defining condition in people with HIV.

Transcription
The step in the HIV life cycle when its DNA is used as a template to create copies of its RNA.

Translation
The step that follows transcription, where the genetic information in the RNA is used to build new copies of HIV.

Vaccine
A substance that stimulates the body's immune response to prevent

or control an infection. Researchers are testing vaccines both to prevent and treat HIV/AIDS, but there is currently no approved vaccine.

Viral Load
The amount of HIV RNA in a blood sample, which is an important indicator of the disease's progression.

Virus
A microscopic organism that requires a host cell in order to make more copies of itself. The cold and the flu are both caused by a virus—and so is AIDS.

Western Blot Test
A laboratory technique used to detect HIV proteins in the blood, which is used to confirm a positive ELISA.

Bibliography

Abdullah, Khalil. "Opium, Drug Use Drive Second Wave of AIDS Pandemic." New American Media, April 19, 2007. news.newamericamedia.org/news/view_article.html?article_id=bb9928f1b2c847b4485b957df8aef2b4

Avert. www.avert.org

Fleshman, Michael. "Drug Price Plunge Energizes AIDS Fight." *Africa Recovery, Vol.1,* June 2001, pp. 1–2.

Herbert, Bob. "The Quiet Scourge: AIDS Is Ravaging Blacks in America. *New York Times* January 11, 2001, p. A31.

Hwang, Ann. "Aids Has Arrived in India and China." *Worldwatch Magazine*, January/February 2001, pp. 12–20.

Lyons, Miriam. "The Impact of HIV and AIDS on Children, Families and Communities: Risks and Realities of Childhood during the HIV Epidemic." UNDP HIV and Development Programme, Issues Paper #30, 2007.

O'Leary, Dale. "AIDS and Sexually Transmitted Diseases Among Men Who Have Sex with Men: Review of the Literature." Fathers for Life. fathersforlife.org/dale/aidsindx.html

Reddy, Sanjay G. *How Not to Count the Poor*. New York: Columbia University, 2005.

UNAIDS. "AIDS Epidemic Updates," December 2003, December 2004, December 2007

———. "HIV and AIDS-Related Stigmatization, Discrimination and Denial: Forms, Contexts and Determinants," June 2000.

UNAIDS, India. "HIV and AIDS-Related Stigmatization, Discrimination and Denial," August 2001.

United Nations Department of Economic and Social Affairs/Population Division. *The Impact of AIDS*. New York: United Nations, 2004.

Index

abstinence 24–25, 68, 75–76
antibodies 8, 11, 92–93, 95, 97, 103
apartheid 68, 70
AVERT 44, 91

Bono 82–85
Brazil 49, 68, 75–78
breast milk 16–17, 40, 92

condom 16, 18, 23–25, 60, 76–78, 86
culture 26, 28–30, 35, 37, 44, 78

discrimination 35, 38, 48–50, 52, 71, 78

Easter 31
education 15, 25, 35–36, 44, 50–52, 63, 74–75, 79, 82, 86

hemophilia 15, 18–19, 96
heroin 43, 46
homosexuality 10, 14, 40–41, 44–47, 75
honor killings 26, 30

immune system 10, 12–13, 92–94, 96–100

Live 8 84–85

malnutrition 59
migration 48, 63
myth 32

nongovernmental organizations (NGOs) 68, 77–78, 80, 82–83, 89

pandemic 7, 54, 56–57, 64, 108
PEPFAR 71, 73
poverty 2, 7–8, 21, 52, 54, 56–57, 66, 74, 79, 82, 86–89
pregnancy 17, 23, 32
promiscuity 40, 44–45

religion 26, 28, 30–31, 44

semen 16, 22–23, 38, 40, 45
sexual intercourse 16, 23, 60
slavery 32, 82

T cell 11, 93–94, 98, 100, 106
tradition 32, 45
transfusion 18, 86

UNAIDS 16, 52, 59, 71, 80
United Nations 48–49, 52, 56, 66, 78–80, 82, 89, 91, 109

vaccines 18, 21, 106–107

Picture Credits

Dreamstime.com:
- 9: Sebastian Kaulitzki
- 11: Sebastian Kaulitzki
- 12: Sebastian Czapnik
- 14: Meckfisto
- 17: Yuri Arcurs
- 18: Nemiro Vyacheslav
- 19: Marianmocanu
- 21: Dietmar Temps
- 27: Aprescindere
- 28: Mailis Laos
- 29: Heidi Tuller
- 31: Lunamarina
- 33: Arne9001
- 34: Akiyoko74
- 39: 578foot
- 40: Tatiana Amrein
- 41: William Rothstein
- 42: Putnik
- 43: Victoria Alexandrova
- 45: Denis Pepin
- 46: Drizzd
- 48: Racorn
- 50: Andreiorlov
- 55: Marko Vesel
- 57: Drazen Vukelic
- 58: Elena Yakusheva
- 61: Ragne Kabanova
- 63: Lucian Coman
- 64: Aprescindere
- 69: 4keeps
- 70: Matt Fowler
- 72: Lucian Coman
- 74: Lucian Coman
- 77: Edward Marques-mortimer
- 80: Leo Bruce Hempell
- 83: Aprescindere
- 84: Imagecollect
- 85: Carrienelson1

20: World Health Organization | WHO.int
79: Sérgio (Savaman) Savarese | Flickr Creative Commons

To the best knowledge of the publisher, all other images are in the public domain. If any image has been inadvertently uncredited, please notify Village Earth Press (www.villageearthpress.com), so that rectification can be made for future printings.

About the Author

Sheila Stewart has written many educational books for young people. She lives in upstate New York with her two children.

About the Consultant

Elise DeVore Berlan, MD, MPH, FAAP, is a faculty member of the Division of Adolescent Health at Nationwide Children's Hospital and an Assistant Professor of Clinical Pediatrics at The Ohio State University College of Medicine. She completed her Fellowship in Adolescent Medicine at Children's Hospital Boston and obtained a Master's Degree in Public Health at the Harvard School of Public Health. Dr. Berlan completed her residency in pediatrics at the Children's Hospital of Philadelphia, where she also served an additional year as Chief Resident. She received her medical degree from the University of Iowa College of Medicine. Dr. Berlan is board certified in Pediatrics and board eligible in Adolescent Medicine. She provides primary care and consultative services in the area of Young Women's Health, including gynecological problems, concerns about puberty, reproductive health services, and reproductive endocrine disorders.

www.ingramcontent.com/pod-product-compliance
Lightning Source LLC
Chambersburg PA
CBHW041959150426
43194CB00002B/61